Organizational Improvement of Nigerian Catholic Chaplaincy in Central Ohio

Towards Effective Collaboration for Rural and Community Development in Nigeria – Ethical Considerations

Organizational Improvement of Nigerian Catholic Chaplaincy in Central Ohio

Towards Effective Collaboration for Rural and Community Development in Nigeria – Ethical Considerations

Hilary C. Ike

Globethics.net Theses No. 36

Globethics.net Theses

Director: Prof. Dr Obiora Ike, Executive Director of Globethics.net in Geneva and Professor of Ethics at the Godfrey Okoye University Enugu/Nigeria.
Series Editor: Dr Ignace Haaz, Globethics.net Publications Manager.

Globethics.net Series 35
Hilary C. Ike, *Organizational Improvement of Nigerian Catholic Chaplaincy in Central Ohio: Towards Effective Collaboration for Rural and Community Development in Nigeria – Ethical Considerations*
Geneva: Globethics.net, 2021
ISBN 978-2-88931-385-3 (online version)
ISBN 978-2-88931-386-0 (print version)
© 2021 Globethics.net

Managing Editor: Ignace Haaz
Assistant Editor: Nefti Bempong-Ahun

Globethics.net International Secretariat
150 route de Ferney
1211 Geneva 2, Switzerland
Website: *www.globethics.net/publications*
Email: *publications@globethics.net*

All web links in this text have been verified as of February 2021.

TABLE OF CONTENTS

LIST OF ACRONYMS AND DEFINITION OF TERMS

ADPC – African Diaspora Policy Center

AU – African Union

CIFA – Center for Interfaith Action on Global Poverty

Diaspora Nigerians – Nigerians living in the U.S.A. or U.S. born children of such Nigerians

EU – European Union

EC – European Commission

EADPD – European-Wide African Diaspora Platform for Development

ECDPM – European Center for Development Policy Management

FBO – Faith-based Organization

First-generation – Nigeria-born but living in the U.S.A or has become a naturalized citizen

GFMD – Global Forum on Migration and Development

ICMPD – International Center for Migration and Policy Development

ILO – International Labor Organization

IOM – International Organization for Migration

JMDI – Joint Migration and Development Initiative

NCCs – Nigerian Catholic Chaplaincies

NCC – Nigerian Catholic Chaplaincy in Central Ohio

PCM – Planned Change Model

RCGD – Research Center for Group Dynamics

Second-generation – U.S.-born with at least one Nigeria-born parent

Social Services Delivery – This include education, advocacy, employment support, healthcare, aid to the poor, rural development efforts, services for immigrants, and so on.

UN – United Nations

UNDP – United Nations Development Program

UNFPA – United Nations Population Fund

UNCHR – United Nations High Commissioner for Refugees

UNICEF – United Nations International Children's Emergency Fund

USA – United States of America

SUMMARY

This research focused on the Nigerian Catholic Chaplaincy in Central Ohio, understood in this study as a diaspora faith-based organization. The hope is that the organizational improvement of NCC will lay foundations for NCC's collaboration with other agencies, towards community development in Nigeria. The theoretical frameworks selected for the research helped to accomplish the research purpose. Scope of the study was limited to first generation members of the diaspora who are Nigerians. First generation refers to members of the diaspora who were born in Nigeria and were at least 16 years old prior to their arrival in the United States.

Acknowledgements

I am grateful to Msgr. Prof. Obiora Ike, my brother and the Executive Director at Globethics.net, for his mentorship all these years. Thanks also to my superiors, Archbishop T. P. Broglio, Bishop C.V.C. Onaga, and Bishop R. J. Brennan, who permitted my academic quest.

Special thanks to my family and friends for their generosity and support which I continue to benefit from in life. Deacon John Crerand and Mother Martha Offor SJGS, deserve some special mention as each of them worked with me at different levels from the beginning to the final production of this study.

1

BACKGROUND OF THE STUDY

This research regards the Nigerian Catholic Chaplaincy in Central Ohio (NCC), viewed as a faith-based organization (FBO) for Nigerian immigrants who are Roman Catholics and reside in the Central Ohio area. The NCC is part of a larger group of Nigerian Catholic Chaplaincies (NCCs) found in various cities of the United States of America (USA). These chaplaincies are FBOs because they constitute a congregation of worshippers drawn to the organization primarily for their spiritual welfare. The group also facilitates social functions that assist its members for better integration into the society. Membership to the NCC is by nationality and adherence to the Catholic faith. There are other non-congregation faith-based service providers organized by Nigerians, recognized by the law as FBOs, but the scope of this research is limited to the Nigerian Catholic Chaplaincy in Central Ohio.

Social science research on FBOs have seen some increase since the 20th century (Bielefeld & Cleveland, 2013a; Burchardt, 2013; Hepworth, & Stitt, 2007). Bielefeld and Cleveland (2013a) argued that social science research seemed to neglect the world of religion and religious-based services in the last century. They observed that the neglect is attributable to the acceptance of a modernization framework that became popular among social scientists in the later part of the 20th century (Bielefeld & Cleveland, 2013a). Consequently, FBOs, like the NCC have not received much coverage in social science research. This dissertation contributes to knowledge regarding NCCs as homogenous immigrant groups residing in the USA. It is the hope that an organizationally improved NCC would be a veritable tool for social services delivery, both in the community where the immigrant group resides and in the rural communities in Nigeria. This research provides suggestions for the organizational improvement of NCC as a diaspora organization.

Religious organizations have always provided social welfare and charitable aids since the pre-modern times. Hepworth and Stitt (2007) opined that it is a matter of the nature of their existence since caring for the needy is a Christian ordinance. Government and non-governmental agencies took up this prerogative in the modern era, relegating FBOs to serving only the spiritual needs of people (Bielefeld & Cleveland, 2013a). In recent times, however, a resurgence of collaborative social services delivery between governments, donor agencies, and FBOs has been prompted by international organizations and non-governmental organizations (NGOs) (Bielefeld & Cleveland, 2013b; Burchardt, 2013; Rogers, 2009). A team of researchers conducted a comparative study on the effectiveness of FBOs over NGOs in Nigeria (Davis, Jegede, Leurs, Sunmola, & Ukiwo, 2011). The researchers set out to establish whether there was significant advantage in using FBOs rather than NGOs for social services delivery. Their study "did not find significant differences in the development-related aims, values, and activities of organizations self-identified as FBOs or NGOs…differences between them were rather evident with respect to programme design" (Davis et al., 2011, p. 2). Nonetheless, research showed that FBOs tend to succeed more than NGOs as providers of social services mostly because they are selective in their types of services and have more volunteers than NGOs (Bielefeld & Cleveland, 2013b).

However, congregational FBOs, like the NCC, lack the organizational structure to partner effectively with NGOs and other international bodies due to their religious-oriented structure. Consequently, other noncongregational FBOs take up these roles although they frequently failed in delivering social services to places that needed them. NCCs focus on the spiritual needs of members and try to create the community life that helps diaspora Nigerians to achieve accelerated social integration. They engage in humanitarian activities as faith-based organizations and use volunteers to render cost effective services as well as mobilizing diaspora contribution towards community development. The NCC in Central Ohio tries to do the same thing. The organization obtained a tax-exempt status in 2014 and have raised up to $30,000 between 2015 and 2018, in preparation for more proactive roles in social services delivery. Annually, the NCC has provided school backpacks for about 100 children since 2014 and wants to embark on charity missions to less privileged communities from 2020. Capacity building and organizational improvement of the NCC will further help to build effective partnerships with donor agencies and international organizations for better provision of social services to the intended areas.

The circumstances that prompt people to emigrate has been a social phenomenon in human society, prompted at various times by different reasons, such as, war, famine, exploration (Castles & Miller, 2009). Economic and human development reasons form the background to diaspora Nigerians' emigration to the Western world. Immigrants from Third World countries mostly gravitate towards the Western and more developed First World countries due to economic impoverishment, poor healthcare systems, political instability, among others (Gordon, 1998). Consequently, diaspora communities have increased as the effects of underdevelopment continues to affect these Third World countries (Castles & Miller, 2009). Great Britain colonized Nigeria but the nation has continued in a downward spiral at various facets of development since her independence (Enyi, 2014; Raheem & Bako, 2014; Udu & Onwe, 2016). International organizations have raised funds from developed countries to assist underdeveloped countries and such social relief packages get to Nigeria. The intentions for the funds were to assist in the different aspects of development and humanitarian needs, but only a minimal amount of those funds finally got to the neediest of that population (Enyi, 2014; Raheem & Bako, 2014). Worse still, the aftermath of colonial domination and exploitation have continued to plague economic and political development in Nigeria, acting as the basic forces for contemporary underdevelopment (Enyi, 2014). Foreign assistance often arrives as spontaneous international aids, which do not promote any sustainable development (Udu & Onwe, 2016). The impoverished communities eventually return to a state of poor health conditions or lack of basic social amenities when the specific international aids have been exhausted (Enyi, 2014; Udu & Onwe, 2016).

In recent times, FBOs have become more involved in the humanitarian efforts to assist the underdeveloped nations (Bielefeld & Cleveland, 2013b; Burchardt, 2013). The U.S. Agency for International Development (USAID) and the United Nations (UN), have acknowledged that FBOs have dedicated themselves more frequently to the delivery of aids to the neediest areas in the population than ever before (Burchardt, 2013; Rogers, 2009). There is greater trust and right intention in the faith-based groups that cause collaborations with international organizations to be more effective. FBOs have the shared values of compassion and service, which motivate their orientation towards community development and propel them into providing social support and relationship structures that build up social capitals, which are invaluable for community development (Hepworth & Stitt, 2007). This study focused on NCC as an FBO in the diaspora, and ways it can help in community development.

Statement of the Problem

Nigerians are people of a deeply religious culture and gathering to worship as a community is integral to their coping mechanism as they pursue their life goals and try to achieve social integration in the society where they reside. Nigerian Catholic Chaplaincies (NCCs) are places Nigerians gather for worship. Members enjoy the spiritual benefits of gathering to worship but there are other needs of the people like, jobs, housing, children's education, skill acquisition, and other social needs that the chaplaincy does not provide. The problem is that the NCC focus only on its spiritual role to the community while members have other needs. There are human resources among the NCC that could help but the organizational structure and the culture in place ought to change for the NCC to play these social roles for members without losing the faith-oriented identity of the organization.

In addition, Nigerians in the diaspora support rural and community development efforts like, building schools and clinics, constructing roads and providing clean water supplies to local communities. Some-times, their remittances fail to achieve the intended goals due to mis-management or subversion of funds by those entrusted with its care. Turner and Kleist (2013) observed that some element of mutual distrust remains between diaspora organizations and governments in their states of origin due to mismanagement of diaspora contributions to homeland development. Creating modalities for diaspora engagement and harness-ing the philanthropy of diaspora Nigerians and other donor agencies toward homeland development is a problem.

Purpose of the Study

The purpose of the research was to propose best practices for the Ni-gerian Catholic Chaplaincy in Central Ohio (NCC) and to help it collab-orate effectively with NGOs and international organizations for social services delivery and community development. The research explored organizational improvement patterns that would affect organizational changes in the NCC toward meaningful contributions to community development while maintaining the organization's faith-based orientation. To accomplish the organizational improvement of a diaspora group, this research focused on those enshrined values of an ethnic community as a necessary step for deeper understanding of its culture.

Research Questions

The following research questions guided the study:

- RQ1: In what ways can one improve NCC organizationally, as a diaspora FBO, for more proactive roles in homeland community development?
- RQ2: How can NCC continue to fulfill the spiritual needs of members and still play major roles in social services delivery.
- RQ3: How can the diaspora NCC attain better organizational structure to collaborate more with other NGOs in social services delivery towards homeland community development.

Significance of the Study

The theoretical significance of this study is its projected contribution to knowledge regarding diaspora FBOs and Nigerian Catholic Chaplaincies in particular. The study offers ethnographic knowledge that would aid future research on the improvement of diaspora FBOs. Its practical significance is that the application of autochthonous African theories and organizational development concepts, as suggested in this research, would improve organizational performance of NCCs for better social services delivery in support of community development, both in the societies of their residence and origin societies. The study is also significant for Governments, NGOs, and international organizations who can benefit from findings in the research for better collaboration with diaspora groups towards rural and community development.

Theoretical Framework

The conceptual frameworks of this research were the Lewin's Planned Change Model (PCM) or Action Research, and Social Transformation Theory (STT). PCM, when applied to an organizational setting, is the foundation for organization development (French & Bell, 1999). Lewin developed PCM in 1946 at an Inter-Group Relations Workshop, organized at the state Teachers College in New Britain, Connecticut, co-sponsored by the Research Center for Group Dynamics (RCGD), which Lewin founded in 1945 (French & Bell, 1999). I will discuss the history and development of these conceptual/theoretical frameworks in a detail in Chapter II.

Lewin's change model argued that observable behavior in an organization is often the result of two groups of forces: the force pushing for change and the force that strives to maintain the status quo (Lewin, 1951). PCM concluded that when both sets of forces are about equal, current behaviors are maintained, while, a decrease in the forces maintaining the status quo produces less tension and resistance, thereby bringing about the desired change in an organization (Lewin, 1951). Change is therefore a modification of those factors that keep a system's behavior stable. The change process itself requires a three-stage process of *unfreezing* (the old behavior), *moving* (to a new level of behavior), and *refreezing* (stabilizing behavior at the new level) (Lewin, 1951). These action steps are the frameworks on which a general understanding of organizational change and future models of organization development were based (Cummings & Worley, 2009; French & Bell, 1999).

Planned change is a distinctive feature of organizational development and its origins are traceable to Lewin's field theory and action research (Coghlan & Brannick, 2014). Organizational development (OD) is the process by which organizations move from their present state to some desired future state (Thompson, 2008). It usually involves a process of planned change, using behavioral sciences to increase organizational effectiveness (French & Bell, 1999). The Nigerian Catholic Chaplaincy, the focus of this research, represents an organization needing this planned change process to move from its current situation to a new level of organizational behavior. Change processes can be discomforting as they create anxieties during the unfreezing stage. In addition, during the moving stage individuals experience cognitive restructuring which they integrate into the new behaviors that the refreezing stage stabilizes (French & Bell, 1999). I chose the theory of Planned Change Model as my conceptual framework because it is the foundation of other models and organization development theories. Applying the theory to the organizational improvement of NCC would help to achieve the research purpose. Another change model that developed from PCM was the Positive Model (PM) or Positive Change Model, which focused on what the organization is doing correctly and building upon those positive capabilities to achieve better organizational outcomes (Cummings & Worley, 2009). These development change models formed part of my conceptual frameworks as I explored the best approach to organizational improvement of a faith-based diaspora organization.

Social Transformation Theory (STT), on the other hand, is a social science theory on which the phenomenon of migration and subsequent diaspora members' tendency for homeland development is based (Castles, de Haas, & Miller, 2013). STT is dependent on the resulting ethnic and racial diversity that migration creates, often leading to fundamental social transformation, different from gradual or incremental changes over a period (Khondker & Schuerkens, 2014). The theory explains the balance effects of emigration and later remittances from the diaspora on the origin societies. This manifests in the hope created by diaspora migrants that the money and knowledge they accumulate abroad could foster human and economic development in their countries of origin, but this is not without credible concerns about brain drain (Castles et al., 2014). Brain drain is the migration of experts or professionals both within countries and across international borders, in search of better standards of living and quality of life (Dodani & LaPorte, 2005). The impact of these migrations of talents on the receiving society increases overtime as the settlement of migrant groups and the formation of ethnic minorities gradually influences changes in the social, cultural, economic, political, and even the religious fabrics of the host society (Castles et al., 2014; Khondker & Schuerkerns, 2014).

Researcher's Lens

The selection of a theoretical perspective (lens) in research is not fortuitous because there are presumptive a priori assumptions for every researcher that influence choice of research. These basic assumptions or theoretical perspectives ultimately become the lens through which the researcher conducts investigations about a research topic (Guba & Lincoln 1994; Maxwell, 2005). Qualitative researchers are increasingly making use of theoretical lens or researcher's lens to guide their study (Creswell & Creswell, 2018). My dissertation study is an ethnographic research on a homogenous group, the Nigerian Catholics in Central Ohio. Ethnography relies on interpretive rather than positivist perspective about the nature of reality (Creswell & Creswell, 2018; Hesser-Biber & Leavy, 2011).

Therefore, my researcher's lens in this study was the interpretivist philosophical perspective. Interpretivists maintain that the social world is constantly under construction through group interactions and interpretations of social reality through the perspectives of social actors enmeshed in meaning-making activities (Hesser-Biber & Leavy, 2011). The interpretive approach focuses on imaginative understanding of the studied phenomenon which includes the researcher's and the respondent's interpretation of reality (Charmaz, 2006). Because this research is an ethnography, the researcher in ethnographic study immerses himself or herself into the world and culture of the participants, sometimes for many years, as both parties mutually try to understand the phenomenon around them (Charmaz, 2006; Locke, Silverman, & Spirduso, 2010).

My role as a researcher in the study was a participant observer since I belong to the group under study as a first-generation Nigerian immigrant. As the Chaplain of Nigerian Catholics in Central Ohio, I had access to the diaspora community and used the interpretivist approach to engage in interviews and observations of the community's life.

2

REVIEW OF LITERATURE

The review of literature focused on literature surrounding the topics of diaspora and homeland development, faith-based organizations, international and non-profit organizations and organizational development. This review of literature occurred under four themes or sections that are the major strands of literature for the dissertation. The first section addressed literature that reviewed the conceptual/theoretical frameworks of the dissertation, while the second theme was on diaspora and homeland development. The third section focused on faith-based organizations and the fourth section was on international and not-for-profit organizations, their collaborative roles toward development. The summary reflects the implications of findings in the reviewed literature.

Theoretical Frameworks

Planned Change Model or Action Research

The Planned Change Model (PCM) or Action Research concept was developed by Kurt Lewin, a "practical theorist" and the intellectual father of the modern discipline of social psychology (Levine & Hogg, 2010). His change model has provided the general framework on which the understanding of organizational change and development could be based (Cummings & Worley, 2009; French & Bell, 1999). Lewin was born in 1890, of Jewish origin, in a German village that is now part of Poland (Levine & Hogg, 2010). He was educated in Germany and obtained his doctorate degree in 1914 shortly before the beginning of World War I (Levine & Hogg, 2010). He served in the military before he suffered an injury and spent nearly a year recovering in a hospital (Levine & Hogg, 2010). His experiences growing up as a Jew in an anti-Semitic society influenced his view of human behavior and his focus on group processes (Levine & Hogg, 2010). Lewin fled Nazi Germany in 1934 amidst rampant discrimination and he immigrated to the United States (Levine & Hogg, 2010). His academic development was influenced by the Gestalt theorists, and coupled with his growing up experiences, Lewin pioneered the development of field theory, a framework for understanding human behavior in relation to social environments of the individual (Levine & Hogg, 2010).

Action research was the means Kurt Lewin devised to apply some of the psychological ideas from the field theory into a practical endeavor (Adelman, 1993; Levine & Hogg, 2010). Lewin and his students conducted quasi-experimental tests in factory and neighborhood settings to demonstrate the greater gains in productivity and in law and order, respectively, through democratic participation rather than autocratic coercion (Adelman, 1993). In action research, Lewin pursued the course of social justice by trying to raise the self-esteem of minority groups to help them seek independence, equality, and co-operation (Adelman, 1993). This was based on Lewin's belief that social problems should be central to the concerns of psychologists, and that, to understand a phenomenon, one had to try to change it (Levine & Hogg, 2010). No action without research and no research without action were Lewin's views that he promoted through action research by the systematic study of social problems and its solution (Levine & Hogg, 2010).

The initial ideas about Action Research or PCM were set out in 1934 and gained a wider audience when Lewin presented it in 1946 at an

Inter-Group Relations Workshop organized at the State Teachers College in New Britain, Connecticut, co-sponsored by the Research Center for Group Dynamics (RCGD) founded in 1945 by Lewin (Adelman, 1993; French & Bell, 1999). Action research or PCM is rooted in the principles of group dynamics wherein change process occurred by phases: Unfreezing, Moving, and Refreezing (Adelman, 1993; Cummings & Worley, 2009; French & Bell, 1999). For Lewin, change process in an organization begins with creating the perception that a change is needed, then moving toward the new desired level of behavior, and finally solidifying that new behavior as the norm (Hartzell, 2018). Lewin explained this change process in the organization using the analogy of changing the shape of a block of ice (Mind Tools, 2018). If you have a large cube of ice but realize that what you want is a cone of ice, you must first melt the ice to make it amenable to change (unfreezing stage). Then you will mold the iced water into the shape you want (moving stage), and finally, you must solidify (refreezing stage) the new shape (Mind Tools, 2018). Freezing usually involves reducing those forces maintaining the organization's suboptimal level. Moving entails shifting the organization's behavior to a new level and refreezing is the process of stabilizing the organization at a new state of equilibrium (Cummings & Worley, 2009; French & Bell, 1999).

The history of organizational development is inextricably related to the early works of Lewin and other contributors to behavioral science (French & Bell, 1999). Organization development, like Action Research, involves a process of planned change, using behavioral sciences to increase organization effectiveness (French & Bell, 1999). Thompson (2009) described organizational development as a process by which organizations move from their present state to some desired future state. The Inter-Group Relations workshop that was held at the State Teachers College in New Britain, Connecticut, in 1946, was a springboard for the Action Research Model of Kurt Lewin (French & Bell, 1999). The Connecticut Interracial Commission and Lewin's Research Center for Group Dynamics based then at MIT sponsored the workshop (French & Bell, 1999). Organizational development evolved from this laboratory training that involved unstructured small-group situations in which participants learned from their own actions and the developing dynamics of their groups (French & Bell, 1999). Lewin's field theory and his concepts about group dynamics, change processes, and action research, fundamentally gave rise to what would later become the various stems of organizational development (French & Bell, 1999).

Organizational development as a term was a recent coinage that emerged simultaneously in the works of Robert Blake, Herbert Shepard, Jane Mouton, Douglas McGregor, and Richard Beckhard (French & Bell, 1999). These behavioral scientists continued the concepts of Lewin's T-Group to coin other phrases like the *development group* or the *group psychotherapy* (French & Bell, 1999). A combination of these groups became "organizational development" group to distinguish them from the complementary management programs that were prevalent at the time (French & Bell, 1999). Nevertheless, action research remains a distinctive feature of organization development and one of its core origins (Coghlan & Brannick, 2014). The pioneering efforts of Lewin which insisted that it was not enough to try to explain things but one also must to try to change them, led to organizational development concepts, namely, that changes in human systems can only be successful if one involves the members of the system in a collaborative inquiry and intervention for change (Coghlan & Brannick, 2014).

Social Transformation Theory

Social Transformation Theory (STT) is the general framework that informs the phenomenon of migration and subsequent diaspora tendency for homeland development (Castles, 2010; Castles & Miller, 2009; de Haas, 2010). STT is about the fundamental changes in society due to the ethnic and racial diversity that migration creates when two cultures meet. Castles and Miller (2009), as well as Khondker and Schuerkens (2014), contrasted this fundamental transformation in society from mere social changes that are gradual or incremental over a period. The authors traced the phenomenon of social transformation to time immemorial since philosophers and sages began to contemplate the modalities and causes of social change in the human society (Castles & Miller, 2009; Khondker, & Schuerkerns, 2014). STT encompasses a wide range of institutional and cultural changes that occur in the society throughout history, especially when two cultures meet and integrate varying elements of each culture with the other (Khondker, & Schuerkerns, 2014). Khondker and Schuerkerns (2014) gave an example with colonialism where two different social systems confronted one another, but not on equal terms. The forces of coercion subdued the natives, making the social systems of the dominant power to become universal values for the dominated (Khondker, & Schuerkerns, 2014).

Therefore, the social transformation phenomenon usually begins with migration, whether for the purposes of exploration or the search for a better life. A true understanding of modern societies is in the conceptual framework of migration studies, linked to social transformation theory as its central category (Castles, 2010). In their research on the age of migration, Castles and Miller (2009) described the challenges of global migration:

A defining feature of the age of migration is the challenge posed by international migration to the sovereignty of states, specifically to their ability to regulate movements of people across their borders. The extensiveness of irregular (also called undocumented or illegal) migration around the world has probably never been greater than it is today. Paradoxically, efforts by governments to regulate migration also are at an all-time high and involve intensive bilateral regional and international diplomacy. (p.3)

The theory of social transformation facilitates the understanding of the complexity, interconnectedness, and variability of such social systems in the multi-level mediations of migration processes within the context of global transformation (Castles, 2010; Khondker, & Schuerkerns, 2014).

Furthermore, Castles and Miller (2009) explained that transformation goes beyond the continual processes of social change to imply such fundamental changes in the way society is organized. The authors attributed this to radical shifts in dominant power relationships and cited the recent massive shifts in economic, political, and military affairs as representations of such fundamental change (Castels & Miller, 2009). The search for higher salaries, access to better technologies, and overall better standard of living causes people to migrate from their societies of origin, creating concerns about brain drain in that society, but soon enough, remittances and development efforts from the people living in the diaspora restore hope for the origin society (Castles & Miller, 2009; Dodani & LaPorte, 2005). The social transformation impact on the receiving society becomes more apparent in the long run as the settlement of migrant groups and the formation of ethnic minorities fundamentally changes the social, cultural, economic, political, and even the religious fabrics of the host society (Castles & Miller, 2009; Khondker & Schuerkerns, 2014). Changes induced by different colonial systems, for instance, influenced the local societies because these societies, willy-nilly, allowed different cultural models to coexist with their individual societies, giving rise to social structures with imposed roles and a resultant social transformation over time (Khondker & Schuerkerns, 2014).

In modern migration, social integration of immigrants into the host country becomes vital for the achievement of a cohesive state as the sending state and the receiving state both stand to gain by the successful integration (Gsir & Mescoli, 2015). After all, the search for higher salaries, access to better technologies, and overall better standard of living prompted modern migration to post-industrial societies (Castles & Miller, 2009). Gsir and Mescoli (2015) agreed that technology and newer means of communication, like the social media apps (Facebook, FaceTime, Twitter, WhatsApp, etc.), have significantly affected the way migrants interact with countries of origin. People and their families back home can now communicate in real time, engaging in politics and influencing economic propositions while remaining in diaspora (Gsir & Mescoli, 2015). It behooves governments and non-governmental bodies to be cognizant of this reality while developing policies for immigration and integration.

Diaspora Organizations and Homeland Development

Migration is not something new, as human beings have always moved in search of new opportunities, often leading to chains of migration (Castles & Miller, 2009). As significant number of migrants settle at a destination, migration becomes self-perpetuating, creating the social structure to sustain the process (de Haas, 2010; Williams, 2010). In one of the early studies on the new wave of African immigration to the United States, Gordon (1998) observed that both labor and refugee migration from Africa to the United States have become widespread phenomena as growing numbers of Africans entered the global stream of international migration. Despite the new diaspora that is the recent influx of African immigrants to the United States, there is limited study of the phenomenon (Gordon, 1998; Williams, 2010). Five major factors account for the patterns in African migration: globalization and integration of the world economy, economic and political development failures in Africa, immigration policies in the US, Anglophone background, and historical ties of sending countries to the United States (Gordon, 1998).

ADPC (2010, 2012) and the International Center for Migration and Policy Development (ICMPD) (2013) reported that international organizations, like the UN and European Union (EU) have been collaborating more with diaspora institutes and not-for-profit organizations to improve the intersections between migration and development. Similarly, diaspora institutes and host country migration policy centers are providing enabling platforms for African diaspora in Europe and in the United States, to pool their resources for the development benefits of Africa (ADPC, 2010; Tinajero & Sinatti, 2011). Growing numbers of African diaspora organizations and entrepreneurs in various countries across the globe are now leading development-related projects largely in villages and rural areas all over Africa (Aman, 2014; Budabin, 2014; Ojo, 2012). These organizations are notably useful in fragile, post-conflict countries that need development assistance, responding to vital needs not met by the development efforts of more established development agencies (Aman, 2014; Budabin, 2014). There remains a mutual distrust between diaspora organizations and governments in their states of origin, as bureaucracies, schemes, and modalities for diaspora engagement in homeland development often becomes politicized (Turner & Kleist, 2013).

Diaspora organizations have increasingly become necessary agents of development because of significant amounts of resources and remittances they send back to their countries of origin for development programs (Kessing & Marquard-Busk, 2014; Newland, Terrazas, & Munster, 2010). Due to their history and purpose, diaspora organizations attract more donors in their host countries for homeland development programs (Kessing & Marquard-Busk, 2014; Turner & Kleist, 2013). Moreover, philanthropy has grown to higher levels in diaspora organizations, with individual donors focusing on strategic giving, aimed at bringing social changes and influencing policy (Newland et al., 2010). These remittances, though at a private sector level, have come to include collective remittances for a common goal in which the philanthropists are the major stakeholders (Newland et al., 2010). A study of diaspora Africans in Germany revealed how individual remittance to countries of origin positively affected economic growth in migrants' countries as well as migrants' host countries (Awojobi, Tetteh, & Opoku, 2017). Awojobi et al. (2017) argued that in a study of Nigerian immigrants to the United States, at least 25,000 Nigerian-born medical doctors are contributing to the health care system and economic growth of United States through their profession and tax remittances.

Members of the diaspora are significant agents of change, both when acting as individuals and when pooling resources together as an organization for the development of their countries of origin (Aman, 2014; Awojobi et al., 2017; Budabin, 2014; Ojo, 2012; Terrazas, 2010; Turner & Kleist, 2013). Turner and Kleist (2013) argued that donors, governments, and not-for profit organizations are courting these emergent agents of change because of their better knowledge of the homeland terrain and their presumed potential for further involvement in development processes. Agunias and Newland (2012) developed road maps intended to serve as guidelines for engaging diaspora communities in development processes. Specific goals of diaspora organizations may vary with each organization's type, but the common interest is always about strengthening their relations to the homeland and helping with development efforts (Ojo, 2012; Williams, 2010).

In summary, different groups and organizations are playing an increasing role in connecting various diaspora organizations to community development (Aman, 2014). The author gave examples with hometown, ethnic, alumni, religious and professional associations. In addition to that, NGOs, investment, political, and welfare groups also participate in development efforts in Africa. Aman (2014) opined that for diaspora network organizations to reach their full potentials in contribution to the development of their respective countries of origin and countries of residence, they ought to aim at facilitating information sharing to maximize their effectiveness.

Faith-based Organizations

Congregations and other houses of worship form what have predominantly become known as faith-based organizations (FBOs), although other non-congregation faith-based service providers also belong to the category of what research regard as FBOs (Bielefeld & Cleveland, 2013). Generally, social science research has neglected the study of religious-based or faith-based social services providers for a long time (Bielefeld & Cleveland, 2013; Burchardt, 2013; Hepworth & Stitt, 2007). In the pre-modern era, religious organizations provided social welfare and charitable acts before the modern state assumed the prerogative, relegating the faith-based organizations to serving only the spiritual needs of the people (Bielefeld & Cleveland, 2013). However, within the last two decades, scholarly research has documented an unprecedented increase in collaborative social welfare and development programs with FBOs, at the behest of governments, international organizations, and donor agencies (Burchardt, 2013; Rogers, 2009). Bielefeld and Cleveland (2013) found a rapid increase in publications regarding FBOs in 1996 that peaked in 2003 but declined again in 2008. In the 1990s, welfare reform discussions included proposals for government to support religious organizations in their efforts to provide social services and this spurred an increase in academic research on FBOs (Bielefeld & Cleveland, 2013).

Greater recognition is now given to FBOs for their contributions in providing social services like feeding the poor, providing clothes and shelter to the homeless, and other forms of charity (UNFPA, 2009; Vidal, 2001). The United Nations Population Fund (UNFPA) (2009) developed guidelines for engaging FBOs as agents of change and vouched to strengthen its partnerships with FBOs around three key areas: capacity building, knowledge sharing, and advocacy. Community development efforts are being promoted by FBOs, even when their organizational structure may not altogether be adequate for extensive community development (Joshi, Hawkins, & Novey, 2008; Vidal, 2001). International organizations recognize the need to collaborate with FBOs, by understanding that their languages or mode of operation may differ, but the objective is the same, namely, provision of social services to humanity (Duff, 2010; UNFPA, 2009; Vidal, 2001). Generally, FBOs justify their efforts in terms of its religious dimension and they use religious languages in the practice of their work, encouraging volunteers to do the same as religious call to evangelize (Davis et al., 2011).

Capacity building and organizational improvement of FBOs is the hoped-for results of partnerships between governments and non-government organizations with FBOs for effective provision of social services (Joshi et al., 2008). FBOs could become effective service providers in important state programs like, prisoner reentry, urban and low-income housing, healthcare delivery, rural/community development, education, and human capital development (Joshi et al., 2008; Vidal, 2001). The Center for Interfaith Action (CIFA), for instance, is involved in global initiatives for faith, poverty eradication, health, and development, as it builds bridges between faith-based and secular development organizations (Duff, 2010). The 'faith factor,' that is, being motivated by shared values of compassion and service, propels FBOs to lead the way in advancing causes of health and development across the world with a feeling of responsibility to do so (Davis et al., 2011; Duff, 2010). As a matter of their purpose of existence, FBOs provide social support and relationship structures that build up social capitals that are invaluable for community development (Hepworth & Stitt, 2007). The results of an extensive study that examined published literature on health programs in FBOs to determine their effectiveness indicated that, most FBO programs that focused on primary prevention and general maintenance reported significant increases in health awareness (de Haven, Hunter, Wilder, Walton, & Berry, 2004). Stronger engagement of FBOs and greater collaborative roles from governments and donor agencies are necessary to accelerate progress on urgent health needs and social welfare challenges (De Haven et al., 2004; Duff, 2010; Hepworth & Stitt, 2007).

International Organizations, NGOs, and Development

Tinajero and Sinatti (2011) produced a handbook that serves as a framework for the European Commission - United Nations Joint Migration and Development Initiative (JMDI) to portray the high-level partnerships required of international bodies in development efforts. In 2010, the African Diaspora Policy Center implemented a project that aimed at facilitating the participation of diaspora-oriented policymakers in Africa in the Global Forum on Migration and Development (ADPC, 2010). The United Nation (UN), European Union (EU), International Organization for Migration (IOM), United Nations Population Fund (UNFPA), United Nations High Commissioner for Refugees (UNHCR), and International Labor Organization (ILO), co-sponsored the JMDI project, a major innovation in inter-agency collaboration that the United Nations Development Program (UNDP) is implementing (Tinajero & Sinatti, 2011). The wealth of knowledge and expertise, including extensive network from these organizations, ensure successful outcomes in the field of migration and development (Tinajero & Sinatti, 2011).

Gsir and Mescoli (2015) of the Robert Schuman Center for Advanced Studies studied the ways governments and non-governmental institutions in the migrants' origin countries strive to establish transnational bonds and what policies the EU recipient countries are implementing for integration of migrants. The researchers noted that, as of January 2013, around 34 million persons born in the Third World countries were living in the EU, constituting 7% of EU's total population (Gsir & Mescoli (2015). Ojo (2013) confirmed the implications of the above study and estimated that entrepreneurship among Africans in Western societies and the accruing remittances from diaspora communities, account for about 2.6% of Africa's gross domestic product in 2010. African Union has designated the Africans in diaspora as the "sixth region" of Africa, highlighting the burgeoning role of people living in the diaspora in economic and social capital development of Africa (Ojo, 2013).

The African Diaspora Policy Center established a European-wide African Diaspora Platform for Development (EADPD), embarking on various activities to empower Africans in the diaspora as change agents for the development of their countries of origin (Aman, 2014). Majority of such empowerment activities were organizational improvement of multiple African diaspora organizations for better interactions and net-working between them and the creation of platforms for regular ex-change of good practices between them (ADPC, 2013; Aman, 2014). The International Center for Migration and Policy Development, in collaboration with the European Center for Development Policy Man-agement (ECDPM), agreed to give considerable attention to migration and development as inevitable realities by creating intra-governmental policy coherence for positive migration and development (ICMPD, 2013).

In 1994, the international conference that gathered 179 governments in Cairo achieved a landmark in migration and development (ICMPD, 2013). The conference adopted a 20-year comprehensive Program of Action (PoA):

Chapter X of the Cairo PoA, which is concerned with international migration, includes a specific section, which is concerned with 'interna-tional migration and development'. Encouraging more cooperation and dialogue between countries of origin and countries of destination in order to maximise the benefits of migration to those concerned and increase the likelihood that migration has positive consequences for the development of both sending and receiving countries. (ICMPD, 2013, p.22).

Summary

Migration is a phenomenon that has always existed within the human society, orchestrated at different periods in history by events like, wars, famine, natural disasters, political strife, or simply economic adventure (Carnegie Council, 2016; Castles & Miller, 2009; Gordon, 1998). The social transformation generated by migration leads to diaspora conditions, which are inevitable elements in social transformation (Castles & Miller, 2009). Migrants struggle with social integration in their countries of residence as they attempt to hold on to some of their cultural values whilst adapting to the cultures of their host society. Achievement of this synchronization increases the effectiveness of diaspora members' contributions to homeland development (Agunias & Newland, 2012; Rogers, 2009; Williams, 2010).

FBOs create the unifying force that helps diaspora communities to achieve social integration. They are in a position to mobilize diaspora organizations better through humanitarian activities and other social welfare services that they provide. It behooves governments and international organizations to build partnerships with FBOs for organizational improvement of diaspora organizations. Such collaboration will render stronger services to development in the Third World countries and ensure quality social services delivery to the intended areas.

3

METHODOLOGY

This is an ethnographic study of a diaspora African community using qualitative research methodology. The chosen research design was because the study explored the cultural underpinnings of an ethnic community – the Nigerian Catholics living in Central Ohio. The rationale for the qualitative genre was that, rather than create hypotheses about a people's lived experiences, it was better to immerse myself in their world and try to understand their social reality from the participant observer perspective. Qualitative research, in general, explores the social meanings people attach to their experiences, circumstances, activities, and events in their world (Hesser-Biber & Leavy, 2011; Roberts, 2010). Qualitative research is also characterized by, inductive analysis of data, focusing on natural settings, with no attempt to manipulate the environment, and emphasis on words (Maxwell, 2005; Merrigan & Huston, 2015; Roberts, 2010).

Furthermore, in ethnographic research, ethnographers immerse themselves in the target participants' environment and engage with the events, people, cultures, motivations, and activities (Charmaz, 2006; Hesser-Biber & Leavy, 2011). Ethnography has its roots in cultural anthropology where researchers immerse themselves within a culture, often for years (Charmaz, 2006; Locke, Silverman, & Spirduso, 2010). The researcher in an ethnographic study explores an intact cultural group in a natural setting over a prolonged period, collecting mostly observational data from the contextual lived realities encountered in the field setting (Creswell, 2003). My research was an ethnographic study of diaspora Nigerians in Central Ohio area, exploring the broad culture-sharing behavior of the group and how to leverage the findings for collaborative community development.

Research Questions

The following research questions guided my research and provided useful information for the organizational improvement of the NCC.

- RQ1: In what ways can one improve NCC organizationally, as a diaspora FBO, for more proactive roles in homeland community development?
- RQ2: How can NCC continue to fulfill the spiritual needs of members and still play major roles in social services delivery.
- RQ3: How can the diaspora NCC attain better organizational structure to collaborate more with other NGOs in social services delivery towards homeland community development.

Setting

The Nigerian Catholic community in Central Ohio is the main setting for this research. As such, the setting was primarily the worship place of the Nigerian Catholic community at a Church located in Central Ohio. Other venues where Nigerians gathered for events and celebrations, as well as the residences, offices of respondents, and libraries formed parts of the research setting.

Sampling

Qualitative research usually makes use of purposive random sampling to select respondents for research (Creswell & Creswell, 2018; Hesser-Biber & Leavey, 2011). This sampling method helps the research to achieve maximum variation to ensure a wide variety of participants. The idea behind qualitative study is purposeful selection of participants or sites that would be of most help to the researcher in understanding the research problem (Creswell & Creswell, 2018). This dissertation research required respondents with in-depth understanding of the group under investigation. Thus, using purposive sampling to select respondents for the research seemed the best idea. The criteria for the selection were nationality, age, residency, duration of stay in the United States, and membership. As such, participants had to be male or female members of the NCC living in the central part of Ohio and are above 18 years of age. Keeping maximum variation in mind, criteria for selection of participants also stipulated that they must have lived in the United States for at least 15 years. One exception included that one of the participants should be someone who is not yet up to five years in the United States. The idea was that the viewpoints of someone still settling into the society was necessary for this research, in contrast with the experiences of those that have been in the country a longer time.

Consequently, I placed announcements at our community monthly services for interested participants. I chose the first five respondents who met the criteria mentioned above. The Recruitment process was by direct contact with the individuals who met the criteria I listed. The vetting process involved a brief interview over the telephone and in person with interested parties until five respondents that met the above criteria emerged. I contacted them personally when they responded to the announcements and confirmed their willingness to participate in the interviews. I met with three of the participants for the one-on-one interviews and concluded interview arrangements by phone contacts with the other two.

Furthermore, I sought and obtained consent from the eight members of the NCC executive board to have them function as the focus group in this research. The rationale for choosing the executive board as the focus group was because, as elected members of the chaplaincy, they are representatives of the community who have been engaged in brainstorming activities for the progress of the NCC. Moreover, I worked with the same executive board during my mentorship project and we have been exchanging ideas on this research topic. None of the board members participated as respondents for the one-on-one interview. They functioned as the focus group for validation of ideas and data from research findings.

Data Collection

Data collection for this research lasted between July 2018 and June 2019. I collected data through one-on-one interviews, focus group meetings, and direct observations. The interviews lasted between 40 – 50 minutes for each respondent. Only one interview lasted 35 minutes. The focus group meetings served as my 'sounding board' for the in-depth interviews, data analysis, and for member checking. Sounding board refers to a process of validation and member check that lasted throughout the research. I met four times with the focus group in a formal capacity, and each meeting lasted between 1 hour and 1 hour 30 minutes for each session. The first meeting was in July 2018. The second meeting (October, 2018) was scheduled once I had the interviews transcribed and had done the preliminary coding process. Thereafter, I met again with the focus group in January 2019 to discuss the compelling themes that emerged from the research. The final meeting was in July, right before the submission of this research to the dissertation committee. To achieve trustworthiness, I let the focus group study the research findings and the conclusions I made from them.

The Nigerian Catholic Chaplaincy meets every third Sunday of the month for service, so I had the opportunity for two-hour observations of the community during Sunday gatherings for twelve times to make for a 24-hour period of direct observations. There were other events, like Christian wakes at the houses of bereaved members or in the Church. Wakes are social gatherings Nigerians hold before the funeral of a deceased member. The ceremony brings Nigerians together and could last between six and seven hours in the evening. The community had several wake services between July 2018 and June 2019, but I attended seven of them and spent a total of 42 hours conducting direct observations. Additionally, I made observations during religious gatherings and at other social events involving Nigerians in general. There was no obstruction of the normal flow of things or intrusion into people's space during the observations.

I used electronic devices to record the focus group interactions and the one-on-one interviews while I took notes of my direct observations. Then I uploaded the collected data from audio recordings into the computer for transcription. Rev.com was the merchant whose services I used to transcribe the interviews and focus group discussions. It cost one dollar per minute of audio recordings. In addition, I saved the audio files in Microsoft OneDrive application for easier access to the saved data from any device that is internet compliant with Microsoft. Subsequently, I deleted the saved data and destroyed all the audio recordings when the dissertation received final approval.

Protocol

The interview protocol (See Appendix A), in line with semi-structured interview style, contained questions aimed at obtaining a contextual grasp of participants' interpretations of phenomena. The protocol reflected the research questions with additional open-ended questions that allowed participants to express themselves freely while describing their experiences. The protocol also contained questions about participants' demographic data and the length of time they have been in the diaspora. The focus group protocol (See Appendix B) contained general questions aimed at obtaining members' perceptions about my dissertation topic of inquiry. Subsequently, I formulated more questions for the follow up meetings based on the data emerging from the one-on-one interviews. It was at the third focus group meeting, for instance, that I confirmed the compelling themes from data analysis. I also observed NCC members' inter-personal communications with one another, noting their non-verbal communications and behavior during community events.

Procedure

I used the unstructured interview format to obtain data for this research. This format allowed me more freedom for follow-up questions to elicit further views and opinions from the participants. The interviews took place at convenient locations of participants' choice. One of the participants elected to have the interview at his workplace while another participant preferred to meet at my workplace. The other participants chose to meet at the Church where Nigerians gather for worship, another chose the city library, and the other invited me to his apartment. I was happy to meet each person wherever she or he preferred to meet. The focus group meetings occurred at our place of worship in Central Ohio. My direct observations were unobtrusive and generally occurred during our community gatherings.

Data Analysis

Charmaz (2006) noted that the potential problem an ethnographer may have is to see data everywhere and nowhere, gathering everything and nothing. I transcribed the audio recordings of the one-on-one interviews and focus group discussions for coding and further analysis. Coding is the initial step a researcher undertakes in moving from concrete statements in the data to making analytic interpretations by linking what the respondents said to concepts and categories (Charmaz, 2006; Weiss, 1994). The process names segments of data with a label that summarizes and at the same time categorizes each piece of data (Charmaz, 2006).

Weiss (1994) observed that in data analysis, no single method of analysis presentation is the only tried-and-true one rather investigators have different styles based on a studies' requirements and audiences' differences. In this research, I focused on the primary purpose of coding, providing materials for sorting and integration. Then, using the process of horizontalization I grouped and analyzed the coded data. Horizontalization is a process that highlights significant statements from transcribed data, creating clusters of meanings and identifying the overarching themes based on the significant statements (Creswell, 1998). I used the emergent compelling themes to write textural descriptions of participants' responses. I discussed these themes and textural descriptions with the focus group for trustworthiness. The themes helped me to create structural descriptions of the participants' experiences by placing them according to the context and cultural values that influenced how they experienced the phenomenon (Creswell, 2007).

Trustworthiness

Dependability, confirmability, credibility, and indeed, validity, are always in the mind of the researcher while conducting research (Hesser-Biber & Leavy, 2011). However, although credibility in quantitative study depends on instrument construction, the researcher is the instrument in a qualitative research (Golafshani, 2003). In qualitative research also, obtaining validity is not a specific end goal as the researcher's role is to present research findings to competing claims and interpretations of readers (Hesser-Biber & Leavy, 2011).

In this study, I collected data from the field through observations, interactions, and interviews. I constantly used member checking and verification of procedures for reliability and trustworthiness. Member checking is sharing and verifying data, analytic categories, interpretations, and conclusions with members of the group or respondents from whom the data were originally collected (Creswell & Creswell, 2018; Lincoln & Guba, 1985). I used the focus group extensively for peer checking as the group is representative of the community. I believe it is an effective way of addressing dependability, confirmability, and credibility of findings in this ethnographic research.

In qualitative research, member checking helps to improve accuracy of findings, credibility, and transferability of a study (Creswell & Creswell, 2018; Roberts, 2010). The same is true of an ethnographic study if the researcher wants findings from the research to achieve dependability, confirmability, and credibility – in other words, trustworthiness of research findings. I further employed data triangulation by comparing data drawn from the participants, from the focus group, and from my direct observations. Triangulation helps to capture alternative perspectives and multiple interpretations that individuals make about their social reality (Hesser-Biber & Leavy, 2011). In this research, triangulation via the different sources of data collection helped me to develop the compelling themes that emerged from this study.

Limitations

The limited scope of this research borders on the fact that it is not a longitudinal study. It cannot account for the future commitment levels of second-generation members of Nigerians in the diaspora. The study does not predict what would become of the Nigerian Catholic Chaplaincy with a later generation of immigrants and with probably lesser need for an ethnic organization. The research relied on the experiences of first-generation members of the diaspora residing in Central Ohio to arrive at its findings. Consequently, sampling and data collection for the research were limited to Nigerian Catholics who are residing currently in Central Ohio. Again, findings from this research may not be transferable to other Nigerian Catholic Chaplaincies in the United States. It is a qualitative research based on contextual experiences of individuals, which may vary from place to place. Finally, a limitation that was out of my control in the study was the researcher's bias. I tried to present the views of participants and used member check to validate them, but I am also a first-generation immigrant from Nigeria. Nonetheless, I maintained objectivity in my analysis of data to the best of my ability.

Ethical Considerations

I protected the anonymity of individuals involved in the interviews by using pseudonyms and altering the roles and circumstances surrounding the participants' setting. All the participants signed the informed consent forms after explaining the implications of participating in the research to them and assuring them of the protection of their identities. I clearly explained to participants their right to withdraw from participation in the research at any time they felt like doing so in the process. I kept the collected data in a safe place while they were in use for data analysis and I destroyed and deleted them after the approval of my dissertation. I ensured accurate transcription of the interviews and shared the transcribed data with the respective respondents for confirmation before using them in the data analysis. I ensured that my writings did not include biased language or words against the gender, sexual orientation, race or ethnicity of a person in the research reports. I also used member checking for the collected data, giving the respondents opportunity for feedback and validation of data. The focus group, as the executive board of the organization, were the reviewers I used for peer debriefing.

Summary

In consideration of the ethnographic nature of this research, a New York Times article by Zimmer (2016) described how a single migration from Africa went on to populate the world. Zimmer (2016) reported how three different groups of scientists, paleontologists, and geneticists assembled genomes for analysis from the six populated continents of the world. "Examining their data separately, all three groups came to the same conclusion: all non-Africans descend from a single migration of early humans from Africa" (Zimmer, 2016, Section A, p. 1). Although this may be a debated fact, it collaborated the statement that the whole story of human history and civilization is one of migration (Carnegie Council, 2016). Indeed, both plants, birds, and animals migrate as well.

The methodology used to accomplish this research ensured accurate representation of research participants' opinions, using various means to validate them. Selection of participants was purposive based on availability and some listed criteria. Participants' privacy was maintained and collected data were destroyed. The conclusions arrived at from data analysis were discussed with respondents and the focus group. The general body of NCC had the opportunity to read the research outcome after the analysis and final reports on the collected data.

4

DATA ANALYSIS AND RESULTS

This research focused on the NCC in Central Ohio as FBO, its improvement for better collaboration with other faith-based groups or nongovernmental organizations. The research outcome would help the NCC to keep fulfilling the dual roles of rendering spiritual support and social services to its members in the diaspora. This purpose warranted the three research questions: (a) In what ways can one improve NCC organizationally, as a diaspora FBO, for more proactive roles in homeland community development; (b) How can NCC continue to fulfill the spiritual needs of members and still play major roles in social services delivery and (c) How can the diaspora NCC attain better organizational structure to collaborate more with other NGOs in social services delivery towards homeland community development.

Participants were selected using a random sampling method. I selected five members of the NCC that were willing to participate. The criteria were that four out of the five participants were required to be persons who have been in the United States for at least 15 years and one person who had not been up to 5 years in the US. One of the participants who I had initially selected revealed that he has been in the country only for 13 years and not up to the required 15 years. Consequently, I chose another participant to replace him. This report purposely altered participants' names and other personal details, like profession, family information, home address, age, and so on, to protect their identities.

This chapter provides a detailed description of respondent's answers in the one-on-one interviews, with summaries of discussions at the focus group meetings. The chapter opened with reports from the first focus group meeting that was a meeting to ascertain members' views on the interview protocol and the research topic. Following the focus group meeting summary is a summary of each participant's vital statistics. Then, I grouped the responses into categories based on the research questions. There is a matrix associated with this chapter, found in Appendix C. The matrix indicated participants' statements that generated the initial codes. Furthermore, I presented tables that contained some of the responses of participants, indicating from which statements the significant codes were formulated. These significant codes informed some selected concepts that we discussed at the second focus group meeting that gave rise to the compelling themes that emerged. The matrix and the tables contain in vivo coding to ensure that participants' voices were not lost in the analysis of data.

First Focus Group Meeting

The focus group, made up of the eight executive members of the NCC, convened at the Church premises to share opinions regarding my research topic and the one-on-one interview protocol. The members in attendance were Okafor, Evelyn, Ngozi, Anna, Max, Ekene, and Ada. Bernard was absent due to family commitments. I have included the focus group protocol in Appendix B of this study. The protocol guided the meeting but did not limit discussions, as the essence of the meeting was to hear the opinions of members regarding the research topic and choice of questions for the one-on-one interviews.

My research topic resonated well with members of the focus group. Each person was encouraged to comment freely on any part of the interview protocol that he or she preferred. Anna gave this reaction to the question about collective efforts toward development:

"I believe that we, Nigerians, who are here in the United States of America, are a privileged group in the sense of the kind of exposure that we have had and continue having toward resources around us and resources for our own development and resources for helping other people. I think to go by the faith in the God that we serve this should be our motive, to use this opportunity. I feel this is an opportunity for us to look beyond our own needs toward what is possible because of our being here, to help our people in Nigeria. What it will take is love. Love is determination. Love is an action. Love is thinking about others and seeing what we can do very easily, because of our situation, to help other people."

The group generally supported Anna's views, although Okafor remarked that "... sometimes it is really, really hard to help people in Nigeria because there's always issues or some issues about who gets what and who controls what."

Ultimately, the focus group validated the questions I intended to ask the individuals selected for one-on-one interviews, but they did not know the identities of the individuals. Moreover, I have been brainstorming with the focus group, as executive members of the NCC, on issues concerning the advancement of the Nigerian Catholic Community. Unity, love, and peace have been their choice words for the promotion of projects and common goals in the Catholic community. Max added during the group meeting that concrete plans ought to be in place in our community to achieve unity of purpose here in the USA before venturing outside the States for any projects. Evelyn opined that as a faith-based organization, NCC must emphasize the increase of spiritual life among members so that the organization can remain true to its identity even while it seeks to help others. Ngozi, on the other hand, offered that community development efforts should begin here in the United States where we can help in educational development of children and providing social services to less privileged people, thereafter, the NCC can use the experiences gained here to give assistance in Nigeria.

Members of the focus group believed that Nigerians in the diaspora are not here by accident but came to the United States by the will of God. They thought that my research topic would encourage more discussions on how the various Nigerian organizations in the diaspora may begin to collaborate with each other and with other NGOs towards community development in Nigeria.

One-on-One Interviews Report

The one-on-one interview protocol is in Appendix A and contains brief descriptions of each participant's basic biometric data, albeit, with alterations where necessary in order to preserve participants' privacy. The biometrics are necessary because, although certain information concerning age, gender, and annual income are not part of the research question, they are still relevant for understanding the participant's viewpoint.

Vin is a professional who migrated to the United States in 2001 and has been in the States for 18 years. He was born in the early 70s, is married and with a child. Vin makes an annual income of at least $100,000. The charities he and his family are involved in are mostly in the US because they no longer have immediate relatives to care for in Nigeria.

Viber is about 60 years of age. He works with the State of Ohio and has lived more than 30 years in the United States. At the completion of their education in the United States, Viber returned to Nigeria with his wife according to their original plan, to help improve the lot of people there. However, they soon migrated back to the United States when political strife and Nigeria's economy got worse. Viber and his spouse earn up to $100,000 annually in wages. They are involved in community development efforts in Nigeria and belong to organizations that are in the US for such purposes.

Freddick is a senior citizen who retired few years ago from a state job. His annual income is below $100,000. He was born in the early 50s and he arrived in the United States about 38 years ago. He had gone back to Nigeria briefly with his wife and children when he completed his further studies but returned to the United States when living conditions became unbearable, especially for the children.

Winner was a teacher in Nigeria before coming to the United States to complete her Masters' degree program. She came with her husband before 1980 and they have been living the United States since then. She earns an annual salary that is above $100,000, likewise, her husband earns more than $100,000 annually. They spend a lot of money in helping their village community in Nigeria and Winner is involved with various charity organizations that help people here in the United States and in Nigeria. She likes to describe herself 'as wearing many hats', in reference to her job title. Winner had many insights about this research topic. She is currently involved in community development efforts that mirrored what I had in mind as a chaplain of the NCC.

Haifa is the participant who recently arrived in the United States. He is much younger than the rest of the participants, not up to 35 years old. Haifa revealed that he is still unemployed because he wanted to complete some certification examinations, but he arrived from an already developed country where he was working before migrating to the United States. His family is still young, and he has no child yet.

In presenting data from the one-on-one interviews, I made effort to safeguard the voices of participants. For the purposes of clear reporting, I placed their responses in categories based on the relevant research questions. I further created tables to present some of those responses that generated the codes. The matrix attached in Appendix C and the tables in this chapter contain many in vivo coding to ensure that participants' voices were not lost in the analysis. This chapter presented the analysis of participants' responses beginning with categories based on the research questions.

RQ1: In what ways can one improve NCC as a diaspora FBO organizationally for more proactive roles in homeland community development?

In order to elicit detailed responses, I asked participants:

a. What was your purpose and aspirations coming into the United States?

b. Describe your experiences while integrating into the American society.

c. How much link with family and friends back home do people in the diaspora maintain?

d. Do you give to charity in general? What percentage of your annual income?

RQ2: How can NCC continue to fulfill the spiritual needs of members and still play major roles in social services delivery?

In order to elicit detailed responses, I asked participants:

a. What is your perception about NCC? What roles would you like to see the organization play in your life and in the Nigerian Catholic community?

b. Is the NCC currently organized properly to undertake this role?

c. If a spiritual role was included in the responses to #18, what are your suggestions for improvement?

RQ3: How can the diaspora NCC attain better organizational structure to collaborate more with other NGOs in social services delivery towards homeland community development?

To elicit detailed responses, I asked participants:

a. Are you involved in any community development efforts, here in the United States or Nigeria?

b. What is your opinion about collective efforts toward community development in Nigeria by the NCC?

c. As a member of the NCC, in what ways do you think the organization can be improved to perform better towards community development in Nigeria?

d. How can the diaspora NCC attain better organizational structure to collaborate more with other NGOs in social services delivery towards homeland community development?

RQ1: In what ways can one improve NCC as a diaspora FBO organizationally for more proactive roles in homeland community development?

• What was your purpose and aspirations coming into the United States?

It was interesting to discover that four out of the five participants had almost the same answers to this question. They came to study and improve themselves then return to Nigeria to help improve other people. The one participant who had a different response was the recent arrival to the States, Haifa. He said he came to the United States because his wife lived here. However, he also expressed his intention for career development, but not with the view of returning to Nigeria. Winner, who is the earliest arrival among the participants, came to the United States with her husband to attend graduate school for higher education before returning to Nigeria. This pattern of emigration was generally obtainable in the 80's when the Federal government and other institutions in Nigeria would send individuals for further studies or technological training. Many of these individuals came back to take up important positions in various institutions in Nigeria, but the participants in this study had similar negative experiences that forced them to head back to the United States.

Freddick recalled, somewhat somberly, "… unfortunately the country I left wasn't the country I met when I came back." He was referring to Nigeria with depleted social amenities and infrastructure. His children struggled in getting used to the environment, the heat, the constant power failures, noise, water problems, and a struggling economy. He said, "I had to choose between losing my family and losing my job in Nigeria." Ultimately, he chose to quit his job and brought back his family to the United States. The other three participants made their decisions at various stages to return to the United States based on similar reasons.

- Describe your experiences integrating into the American society.

There were varied accounts of individual experiences from the participants' struggles to adapt into the American culture. Viber said "… it was a shock, to say the least," because what he expected was not what he encountered. He opined that nothing could possibly prepare one for an altogether different culture and environment. It was snow and the very cold weather that shocked him the most. He also had not attended college in Nigeria before his arrival and found the teaching methods in the schools here quite different. Winner described a different kind of experiences. She and her husband researched about the demography of United States and determined that the South part of the United States would be their destination. They figured that the South part had more people of African origins. Yet, they suffered the "new arrivals syndrome" of being singled out for their accents and having in turn to struggle to understand the American people's accent. "They couldn't understand what I was saying, so people would start laughing and making fun of you in the classroom," Winner recalled. She went on to recount how, "They say we speak fast [while] I couldn't even take notes in the classroom because the professor spoke too fast." Winner and her husband would later learn to read chapters ahead to be ready for classes. As she recalled,

"… from year three in the university I didn't have any problems, because all those things, chemistry, biology, math, were things we did in high school. It was like kind of refresher for us and the other students began to come closer as they saw the stuff we're made of."

What Winner described as the hardest part of their experiences integrating into the American society when they newly arrived was the limited means of communication with family back home. She almost teared up as she reminisced that, "The hardest part of being here at that time was no communication. And at that time, I had left my only child back in Nigeria." It was only through letter writing that they could communicate, and it took several weeks back and forth.

Freddick had prior biases about the American culture, from the stories he had heard in Nigeria about drugs, shootings, being at the wrong place at the wrong time, and so on. It turned out to be quite a different scenario when he arrived. "They weren't all cowboys shooting everybody else, you know," he chuckled. "I realized how friendly and welcoming the American people are and how they say hi, hi to people they know and those they do not know." This was an amazing experience for him because, according to Freddick, "… we don't do that in Nigeria either." Like Winner, Freddick struggled initially with understanding the American accent. In his description, "I had to get used to the way they speak their English, you know. They hardly pronounce any word that has a 'T'. All their T turns to R. So, when they talk, I had to keep cracking my brain to make sure this T is R or this R is T, you know." However, he claimed to have easily adapted to the American accent in about a month or two.

Vin and Haifa had easier experiences integrating into the American lifestyle as each of them had lived for some years in other developed countries. Vin, for instance, had lived for five years in Europe before his arrival to the United States. Therefore, for him, "… it wasn't much of a big deal." Moreover, as he reassured, "I've been in school environment, professional environment, academic environment and all that." However, he remarked that his initial arrival to Europe was not easy integrating into the society, referring to what he termed "… the liberal Western lifestyles" and their having no "sense of the sacred." Haifa also affirmed that, "… because I have lived in a 'First World' country in the past until I moved here so I think the experiences I had living there is similar because of the level of civilization and culture." Consequently, these two participants did not witness significant challenges while integrating into the American society.

- How much link with family and friends back home do the people in diaspora maintain?

Participants responded in varied forms to this question. The reason for asking the question was to see how much connected they were with people back in Nigeria in order to understand how proactive they may be willing to get involved in community development efforts with the NCC.

Vin, for instance, said that while he was completing his studies here in the United States, the only direct relative he had back in Nigeria was his mother. After having arrived in the United States in 2001 to complete his doctoral studies, Vin's mother died a few years later. Therefore, Vin maintains minimal contact with family and friends back in Nigeria, except for a cousin who communicates with him now and then. Haifa, on the other hand, stated that his relationship with his family and friends back in Nigeria is "… very good and cordial." He reassured that "We are in constant contact. I speak with my family almost every day." Haifa is the participant who has been just a few months in the United States at the time of the interview.

Winner and her husband were able to maintain links with family and friends back in Nigeria through letter writing and sometimes writing checks from their savings in Nigeria to their parents for the upkeep of their child. This relationship has also kept demands from home on the rise especially when the couple finished their studies and got jobs.

Asked how often she made remittances to Nigeria, Winner responded, "When we finish [interview] I will show you my receipt for the money I sent home right before this interview appointment." The respondent said that demand for assistance is constant, but she is grateful to God for the opportunity to help. She described her relationship with family and friends back home as great but reiterated that all the people back home care about is money. Yet, she insisted, "I'm happy to do it… I do it happily, I don't do it grudgingly."

Freddick joked about the period he arrived in the United States referring to it as something that occurred in the last century. He boasted of having put in 23 years of work with the state of Ohio and is now retired. Freddick has good relationship with family and friends back home which he would not want to sever, but he wishes that they would stop being so demanding. When quizzed further about this assertion, he said "… it was like I should solve all their problems for them." The respondent described this as the general mindset of the people back home. Furthermore, Freddick bemoaned the challenges of making remittances, stressing that his relatives have no idea the amount of income tax he has to pay in the US, and that when he deprives himself to save some money from his hard-earned income to send to his people in Nigeria "… they didn't think it is doing enough." He referred to this as greediness on their part because they thought that aid from him was their birthright. Vin echoed similar experience with remittances, saying that people from Nigeria "… bug you with phone calls asking for money… nobody calls you from home to ask how [are] you because they are always asking for money." Winner also agreed with this notion. She said the only friendship the people back home have with you is money and they never ask how you are faring. She noted that even people who are better off than you are will still expect you to send them money and "… if you don't send them money like after two or three months, they say you have forgotten them."

- Do you give to charity in general? What percentage of your annual income?

Viber who earns a 6-digit combined annual income with his spouse said they give above 10% of their income to charity annually. When quizzed about the percentage that goes to family and friends back home, he responded, "This is a tough question because… you know, you get a phone call, and knowing what people are going through back home, we give without minding so to say. It's really hard to quantify it into percentage." He gave a classic example with a call he received recently from a relative who needs to bury a family member. Burial involves money, he explained, "… so I will give and I'm not [gonna] write it down in order to quantify the percentage." He ended by asserting that, "Yes, we do give almost on a regular basis." I asked Viber whether he gives back because he understands what having nothing means. He said yes and proceeded to explain that: "… what inspires me to give and not quantifying or minding what I give is because we grew up in abject poverty." The respondent recounted how he developed the sense of survival from an early age due to poverty and a difficult childhood.

Vin is a professional, whose annual income is above $100,000, excluding his spouse's income. He had explained that he no longer has direct family back home in Nigeria, but occasionally, he gets a call from distant relations. In his words, "Every now and then, there is a death or something like that … and then we send them money." He reminisced when his mother was still living, how he would send 20% of his annual income back home for her sustenance. He observed that although he now sends only about 5% of what he earns annually, it is greater than what he used to send because he is earning much more now than before. Vin described another level of charity that he does through his professional organization. Ethical considerations prevent a total description of this charity, but it involves assistance to people who are not financially able to pay their bills. This form of charity is concentrated here in the US and takes up 10% of his annual income.

Winner is actively involved in doing charity and enthusiastically nodded her head when asked if she gives to charity. She promptly said, "Yes, I do a lot, both here and at home." She announced that, "... every year we give up to $20,000 between me and my husband." Concerning remittances, Winner said, "We are constantly sending money home." Haifa also gives to family and friends back home, although he only arrived newly but he continues to send money home from his savings. He insisted that giving to charity should begin among us here in the diaspora, by people sharing information with one another to facilitate social integration and progress among members. He argued that it is only when members are thriving in their areas that collective efforts toward community development back home will be realized. Haifa suggested the NCC should have an information hub, a website, where members can share resources to help each other.

Freddick's annual income is below $100,000, he said he still gives 10% of his income to charity, which includes remittances to family and friends back home in Nigeria. He also cited death in the family or a relative's family as unavoidable occasions that warrant making remittances. I asked him if funeral rites cost so much in the African setting and he said it could cost him "... like three thousand, five thousand, you know." Freddick reiterated that as an elder, "... because I know the culture, I have to do something. Because my name is on the line, being the first child in the family." I further inquired how his self-image and name could still be so important to him after living so many years in the United States. Freddick responded, "... um, because I grew up in that society, you know, so it's very important to me, you know. It's like you're nobody if you don't meet some of these expectations... a write-off." He reasoned that such charities are important for the preservation of one's integrity, image, and respect. He concluded that, "Those are the needs you need to meet at home if you must belong there." I asked if his children born and raised in the US have such needs back home. He said, "No. my children here are more 'Americanized' and I am trying to 'de-Americanize' them to an extent, to have some Nigerian thing in them."

RQ2: How can NCC continue to fulfill the spiritual needs of members and still play major roles in social services delivery?

- What is your perception about NCC? What roles would you like to see the organization play in your life and in the Nigerian Catholic Community here in the USA?

Vin's perception of the NCC is from the perspective of the organization's social role in the community. He adumbrated that,

"... we are all immigrants, and we are in a very far far far away land ... So, ... you want to create another home you know, in a foreign place where you come together, you meet, you discuss, you mourn together when something bad happens ... and more importantly, for our children to get to know each other and hopefully grow up together as Nigerians living here."

He drew analogy with the function of an embassy in a foreign land where citizens of that country whose embassy is in a foreign land find a home in their country's embassy abroad. So should the NCC be for Nigerian Catholics living in Central Ohio, according to Vin.

Viber favored the spiritual role as the leading function he would like to see the NCC play in his life. He had described his family background as rich with Catholic traditions, with a priest and a nun in his family. He opined that he would like the NCC "... to continue to strengthen my faith, and our faith in general and that is for us to subscribe very strongly to the teachings of Christ in the Holy Scriptures, to abandon ourselves and embrace God." Viber's perception of NCC is a community that recognizes Jesus Christ among each other and tries to render help to others in self-abandonment.

Haifa, who has been here only briefly, suggested a more social role by the NCC. He would like the organization to provide morale support to members in good and bad times. Information sharing is one way he identified that the community can achieve support to members efficiently. NCC, for him, is "… a community thing that efforts need to be put together to assist one another to grow and to better integrate and assimilate in the society." Winner, on the other hand, thinks that the NCC is not making much progress. She surmised that, "We are not increasing in number, the commitment is low and … Seriously, it's not moving at the rate I think it should be." She also thinks that we are not engaging our youth effectively. The youth are not involved as altar servers and there are no youth programs for them.

Freddick's perception of the NCC was a mixture of spiritual as well as social support system. He expressed contentment that Nigerian priests celebrate Masses in the local dialect, which makes people to feel at home and assuage their nostalgic feelings. "We need to have a little bit of home flavor in the community here, you know," Freddick, quipped. The NCC, for him, affords Nigerians who belong to it that sense of belonging, which is difficult sometimes to achieve in the larger American society. He also thinks that with that sense of belonging and a thriving community, it becomes easier to plan to help people back home in Nigeria.

- Is the NCC currently organized properly to undertake this role?

Freddick believed that the current organization structure of NCC is sufficient to undertake the roles he adumbrated. He stated that in fact, the NCC is fulfilling these roles, and only wishes for an increase in membership. In his words, "Membership drive is one thing that you have to concentrate on, otherwise my social need, my psychological need; they are meeting those ones perfectly right." Winner does not think the NCC's current structure is adequate for serving in the roles she wished NCC to play in the community. She strongly advocated for group-leadership style where different groups oversee various ministries. Then, leaders appointed for each of these groups for accountability.

When asked whether the current organization structure of NCC is sufficient to undertake the roles he wants it to play, Vin opined that NCC is in good shape to do so. His arguments were that, based on where the organization was at the beginning, it has seen tremendous improvement in the last four or five years. Vin, like other participants, bemoaned the paucity of members that turn up for events, but he attributed it to busy schedules and people's efforts to provide for their families. He enumerated the various projects and organizational structure in place that have ensured improvement of NCC. Viber expressed hope in the steps the NCC leadership is taking towards the organizational improvement of the NCC. He did not think the current structure was adequate but emphasized that supporting the leadership and uniting to work together toward common goals will get NCC to its desired goals. Haifa did not have comments on this topic, which he admitted is due to his being unfamiliar with how things are structured, having been just five months in the country as of the time the interview was conducted.

- If spiritual role was included in the responses to #18, what are your suggestions for improvement?

Viber had made spiritual role the central theme of what he expects the NCC to fulfill in his life and in the community. He had said, "I would like the NCC to continue to strengthen my faith, our faith in general…" Retreat was his suggested panacea towards achieving this growth. Viber believes that, "… the more we have retreats … I believe some of the little things that may create division or distraction … we should be able to overcome some of these things." Vin did not think that the NCC should be preoccupied with the aspect of spiritual role. He explained that, "… it's not that the spiritual part is not important but there's a reason why it's called Nigerian." For him, people can always gain spiritual assistance from their parishes, but gathered as Nigerians, it ought to be about promoting the things that make us Nigerians.

Similarly, Winner opined that faith improvement is important but what she cherishes the most about NCC is the cultural dimension to our worship. She described her experiences, "For me, I love it when I come in if you see me in the Church I'm jumping up and down. When I come, I feel like I'm at home in Nigeria … because that part of me is missing." Freddick is all for the spiritual and social roles by the NCC. He had expressed appreciation for the efforts to celebrate the Mass in a Nigerian language and hopes that the spiritual gathering will continue to unite Nigerians for a common purpose. He suggested that the priests keep the people up to date on the holy days of obligation in the Church and other feasts in the liturgical calendar so to ensure active participation by members in the Church's prayer life.

RQ3: How can the diaspora NCC attain better organizational structure to collaborate more with other NGOs in social services delivery towards homeland community development?

- Are you involved in any community development efforts, here in the United States or Nigeria?

The following statement from one of the participants is a good instance of the African person's perception of community development effort:

"I haven't stopped rendering hands if you will. I only stopped my education at the master's degree level, I wanted to obtain a PhD from Ohio State but the nature of the work I was doing then could not let me continue with my program. Nevertheless, my wife and I have been able to train one of my nephews to obtain a PhD from the University of Ibadan, Nigeria, and so, I see it as me now obtaining a PhD from the university. So, I am grateful to God for that (Viber)."

Viber is a member of his hometown's organization in the diaspora, an organization that based in the USA. It comprises 32 families from the same village in Nigeria who reside in the US. They formed the organization as a group effort toward the development of their local community in Nigeria. Viber boasted that, "We provided electricity to the entire village, starting from the poorest areas and finally to the areas where members of our organization have their homes."

Winner is involved with two organizations that are devoted to carrying out charity missions both in the US and in Nigeria. She believes in training people who will help to train others. She also promotes small-scale businesses among the women for self-sufficiency. She and her husband have sponsored many people through the university education.

Freddick listed some non-governmental organizations in the USA that he supports financially as his own contribution to community development. They are mostly in the health sector, like, the Cancer Society, Kidney Society, and Catholic Relief Services. His father had died of kidney problems and himself is a cancer survivor, so he donates to the course of these organizations for health development. In Nigeria, he had tried to contribute to the renovation of a school restroom but lack of accountability by the school administration discouraged his continued support of the project.

Vin is not directly involved with any community development efforts in Nigeria but belongs to an organization that has such ideas in its plans. Haifa relocated recently to the United States and is not yet involved in any community development efforts here, but, according to him, "I intend to in the future." He is full of ideas about community development efforts in Nigeria. He remarked that, "There are a lot of things that our people need back there in Nigeria, most of their needs are not being met by the government." Haifa thinks that the onus is on those in the diaspora "... to supplement those needs by being generous and contributing towards community development in different ways. Maybe, in education, health or even assistance with skills and training and business."

- What is your opinion on collective effort toward community development in Nigeria, by the NCC?

The repeated emphasis on paucity of number in the community events of NCC highlighted Winner's opinion regarding programs of the NCC. She is all for the idea of collective efforts toward community development and said she belongs to an organization that has spent thousands of dollars in aids both here and at home in Nigeria. In addition, on personal basis, Winner runs a project at her village in Nigeria that loans out money to less privileged women for small-scale businesses. The project began with 10 women with the plan that when their businesses stabilize, they can return the loan amount which will be given to others, and so on. Winner's passion is especially for women, elderly people, and children.

Freddick thinks that collective effort towards community development in Nigeria is something worth doing. His concern is that the current structure of the NCC cannot ensure that donations get to the intended places, considering the nature of corrupt practices in Nigeria. He cited an experience he once had when he wanted to construct a restroom for a local school and how the school administration received the funds but never carried out the project. Therefore, Viber concluded that collective effort is something worth doing but the "Nigerian Catholic community has to really plan it well."

Vin concurred that collective effort towards community development "... is great thing to do if we can." He opined that the Church is supposed to be the leader in carrying out aids to people who are less privileged. The problem Vin envisaged was the poor turnout of Nigerians, which reduces the capacity for big development efforts. "But yeah, ideally, if everybody were to come out, that will be a great thing because we will be able to have all kinds of programs, both here and at home to help a lot of people."

In the same vein, Viber agreed that collective efforts towards community development in Nigeria by the NCC would be a noble idea. He stated that,

"It is an ideal thing to do if and only if all of us agreed to make sacrifices because if Christ sacrificed himself for the atonement of our sins ... why can't we make monetary sacrifice or any effort that we can to help the impoverished communities back home in Nigeria?"

Viber suggested that it does not have to be gigantic projects but simple things like, helping to renovate elementary schools, or providing them with chairs and toilet facilities.

Haifa had various suggestions that would ensure a coordinated effort towards community development. He had earlier stated that the people in the diaspora have so much they could do to help each other in the USA and render assistance to people back in Nigeria. He repeatedly stressed on the need to create an information hub where people living in this community could offer information and obtain necessary information for their own growth here in the US. Haifa's belief is that when people are flourishing in their places of residence, then, they will eagerly render assistance to others in Nigeria. Haifa listed various projects that collective efforts could promote, like organizing a free health check for people in the local communities through a team of doctors and health care practitioners among us, putting items together to visit motherless babies' homes, and organizing school materials that to be given to schoolchildren both here and in Nigeria.

- As a member of the NCC, in what ways do you think the organization can be improved to perform better towards community development in Nigeria?

Winner suggested that we develop a survey to find out what members of the NCC want for the organization. This would be the initial step towards finding out ways to improve the organization and the reasons people are not responding to invitations to participate in events. The survey will also find out what time or days of the week works best for people. Once we get the answers to these inquiries, we can set up workshops and create groups that will take charge of different aspects of the organization's missions.

Viber opined that creating committees and entrusting leadership of the committees to various individuals would improve NCC's performance. He gave instance with a development committee that he said would first carry out research to find out what the needs of the people are and establish plans of action on how to meet those needs. Viber also emphasized that organizing retreats and improving the community's spiritual life will help to draw the NCC community closer and in turn increase the charity efforts the organization sets out to achieve.

Freddick's opinion on how to improve the NCC is to align the organizational structure properly. He pointed towards the handling of donations and making sure that accountability is in place before embarking on fundraising. His argument is that when donations are not justly distributed the donors may not be willing to keep giving support to the organization's community development efforts. Freddick, also opined that increasing the number of members of NCC is important for organizational improvement of NCC.

Vin emphasized fundraising and writing of grants as ways of improving the organization's performance in community development efforts. He maintained that NCC's recognition, as a non-profit religious group is essential to the improvement of the organization's performance in community development efforts. The 501(c) (3) tax exemption status that NCC obtained will encourage members and other people to donate money towards the accomplishment of NCC goals. Vin opined the development of other ways of raising funds for projects since our number is small, like writing grants for community development projects here in the US or at home in Nigeria. He suggested that the NCC explore the Bill Gates foundation, the Catholic Foundation in Columbus, Ohio and other such foundations that might be willing to support community development efforts.

- How can NCC be organized to collaborate better with government or not-for-profit agencies (NGOs) towards community development in Nigeria?

Haifa thought that the NCC should not work with the government agencies or NGOs because it could skew the objectives in the process. He is of the opinion that the NCC go it alone and carryout projects only within its capacity. He believes that members of NCC have useful talents and are capable of so many development efforts. He gave an instance with health education, which he believes is very much in need for local communities in Nigeria. Haifa opined that dedicated NCC members could organize health education rallies without the help of other NGOs. He suggested that members of NCC could collectively have a wider outreach and impact rural development in Nigeria if they carry out projects in the name of NCC at their various places of origin. Haifa is confident that Nigerians in the diaspora have the wherewithal for raising funds necessary to impact community development in Nigeria.

Viber belongs to other social organizations here in the US. He admitted that those organizations are still exploring ways of collaborating with NGOs and government agencies. These agencies, for him, could be outside the USA and indeed in any part of the world. Collaboration with such agencies, for Viber, is to tap into their wealth of resources toward funding their organization for community development in Nigeria. He suggested that NCC should use its tax-exempt status as an NGO to seek for grants from big organizations. However, he explained that the organizations he belongs to, carry out development projects in Nigeria through levies imposed on each member and from their annual dues.

Responding to the question on how to organize the NCC for better collaboration with NGOs, Vin opined that NCC ought to look internally for talents and experience. "I think we have professionals," he said, "... and we have talents as members of our community that we have to tap... we have professors, we have medical doctors, we have lawyers and we have all kinds of professionals that belong to our NCC. We just have to use them." Vin strongly believes that rather than try to collaborate with these big organizations, NCC can tap into its own rich talents and channel their resources properly towards community development here in the US and in Nigeria.

Freddick maintained that, as a senior, the NCC is now the only organization he actively belongs to, "... which is both social and religious for me," he added, with a chuckle. I asked Freddick whether there was need for NCC to collaborate with NGOs towards community development in Nigeria, or if NCC should just focus on the community here in the US. His first response was, "I would say charity begins at home." Then, he went on to suggest that the primary objective of NCC at this stage should be to get organized, to increase membership, and then go for fundraising drives. He thought that without an organized NCC channeling the funds properly might be an issue.

I did not get to ask Winner if she considered collaboration with NGOs something worthwhile because, she was full of ideas about some not-for-profit organizations that her women's group has been working with. She said that her group works in collaboration with charitable organizations both here in the US and in Nigeria. They raise funds through these organizations in the United States and carry out charitable works through established NGOs, like the Red Cross, in Nigeria. Winner is currently working on creating a food bank in Nigeria where people who have no means of livelihood could at least get some food to eat.

Significant Codes from Interview Data

I deduced the following codes from participants' interview data. I created Table 4.1 during the data analysis to show a bird's eye view of the codes (see Appendix C). Table 4.1 places these codes side-by-side with the significant statements derived from participants original responses. I noted several preliminary codes on the left margins of each participant's interview transcription from which the following significant codes emerged:

Table 4.1.

Significant Codes

Self-improvement	Community development efforts
Planned/positive integration	Collective effort toward development
Accent challenge and social integration	Tribal sentiment
Sense of independence	Collaboration with NGOs
Sense of entitlement	Spiritual role
Social role	Sense of belonging
Self-determination	Family ties
Charitable spirit	Communal spirit
Organizational structure	Information hub
Self-funded projects	Unrealistic expectations from home
Need for numerical strength	Self-image
Accountability	

These codes came from responses of participants based on the interview protocol. To validate the data from the interviews, I presented the codes shown in Table 4.1 to the focus group. The focus group received the transcribed data and the significant codes one week before our meeting because it was important that they had time to go through the data and review the codes I had developed. Their input influenced some changes to my choice of words for the codes. In addition, as my sounding board, I shared some new concepts with the focus group, concepts that I gleaned from what the respondents seemed to be saying during the interviews. Validation of those concepts with the focus group helped me to develop some themes from the codes.

Second Focus Group Meeting

The first meeting with the focus group had occurred before the one-on-one interviews. In that meeting, I discussed and validated the interview protocol with the focus group that made contributions that guided the one-on-one interviews. The second meeting took place when I had completed and transcribed the one-on-one interviews with participants. The focus group validated my preliminary codes and offered better choice of words for some of the codes I later developed. Therefore, as the group animator, I shared with them those concepts I had developed from recurrent participants' responses. The concepts highlighted some cultural undertones from the interview participants' statements, which I could only pick out because I share the same cultural background with the participants. The focus group, made up of members from a similar cultural background as mine, was necessary to validate my opinions. The concepts are not specific to questions used on the one-on-one interview but covered the generality of responses given by participants. The discussions I had with the focus group would later help in the development of overarching themes for my study. The concepts include, our people; communalism; burying the dead; numerical strength; and culture shock. The following are my observations from the group discussions:

The concept "Our people," which was frequently used by the interview participants, represented some deep cultural meaning. Responses from the group discussion showed that this concept encapsulates the whole meaning Africans placed around the African society, made up of families, tribes, and the larger society. Individuals in the focus group offered their opinions on what it means to them when they hear the expression "our people?" Evelyn (pseudonym) explained that she understands it to mean both her immediate family members and members of her village. She also admitted that when far from her village, "our people" means her entire tribe and she easily refers to people from her tribe as "my people." Ekene agreed with this view and expressed that, as someone living in the diaspora, he refers to everybody from his race as "my people" when talking about them. Anna who is from the Igbo tribe in Nigeria, opined that she regards all Igbos as her brothers and sisters. So, she feels comfortable referring to them as "our people." Max expanded the idea further to include all Africans. He said that from his interactions with other Africans, especially those in the diaspora, "… we easily connect with each other and see ourselves as one." Therefore, the concept of "our people" makes sense, according to Max.

Communalism is another concept that resonated well with participants in the focus group. Ngozi said she grew up in the rural area of Nigeria where people celebrated as well as mourned together. In her little village, Ngozi explained, the birth of a newborn is a cause for rejoicing in the entire village. People would visit the parents of the new baby and rub white powder on their faces from the newborn's baby powder. Then, they will sing songs of joy and congratulations to the parents of the newborn. She explained that when someone dies in the community, the village similarly gathers to mourn with the bereaved family. Okafor concurred with Ngozi's experience, saying that his father was a chief and often convened meetings of the kindred in his compound. I asked Okafor to explain the significance of a chief in his cultural milieu. He said that the closest analogy for a chief in his culture was an elder statesman who commanded great respect in the community. Okafor recounted how the elders would gather at his father's compound for meetings about the good of the community and conflict resolutions between individuals or families. The sense of communalism, in Anna's perception, pervades every area of community life from her own experience. Anna recalled as a young woman when some women of her village would report her to her mother if they saw her in some uncompromising corner of the village with a young man. She pointed out that the raising of a child in her community was everybody's responsibility because her uncle or indeed any elder in the village would instantly correct her if she were doing something wrong. Ngozi chimed in that it was a similar experience for her growing up, even in the urban area, although with less intensity than in the village.

Burying of the dead was among the phenomena the focus group discussed as an inseparable part of communalism. Max, who recently lost his father, attested that he was amazed at the amount of solidarity and support he received during the funeral ceremony of his father. He observed that even people he had not met before were part of the many that donated money and offered various helpful services toward the success of his father's funeral. Ekene said that he was still a little boy when his father died, but that his uncles ensured the success of the funeral rites and visitors were entertained. He recalled as a little child how people kept coming to their house for several days after the burial, bringing gifts of food items and drinks. Evelyn quipped that her parents are still alive, although they are well on in age. She agreed with the opinions of others, saying that she has attended several funerals and would often contribute to support the bereaved family. This aspect of communalism is something that resonated deeply with the focus group. The ones that have not experienced the death of a close family member readily admitted that funeral rite was a community event and members of the community rallied round to support the bereaved both financially and emotionally.

I asked the focus group about the significance of numerical strength among the Nigerian people as all the participants in the one-on-one interviews seemed to bemoan the paucity of NCC population. Evelyn pointed out that other Nigerian diaspora organizations are experiencing the same complaints. She thought that having large numbers in an organization such as the NCC would ensure that the financial contributions members might affect the organization's goals. Okafor added that the Igbo people have a saying, igwebuike, which means there is might in numbers. He opined that due to the communal culture of Africans, numerical strength is very essential to societal growth and development. Ekene agreed with this point of view. He recalled that when the NCC first began, the number of members was so small, and they had to go to Nigerian people's houses to try convincing them into joining the NCC. He concluded that, "… without numerical strength NCC can hardly achieve its goals."

Finally, I inquired from participants what aspects of the new society they entered contributed more to their own culture shock when they first arrived in the United States. Anna immediately recounted her voyage to the United States and the challenges she and her spouse experienced at the early beginnings. The initial shock she experienced, as she recalled, was the individualism and people's indifference to others' situation. Anna recounted, "I had two little toddlers then, but there was no neighbor to leave the children with and go for grocery shopping as you would do in Africa." This aspect of the new society and the challenges it presented constituted Anna's initial culture shock. Max came to the United States as a young student in his early 20's. The university which gave him admission was a little far from the Central Ohio area, meaning that Max had to live in the university area. He recalls that the culture shock he experienced was the 'unbecoming behaviors' of his fellow students. Max explained that, in the part of Nigeria where he came from, premarital sex was often considered a taboo, but, young students in his university were easily "getting hooked up" with one another. Max explained that the permissive culture jolted his hitherto moralistic sense of the sacred.

Ngozi said she did not experience much of a culture shock because of her younger age when she arrived in the United States. She gained admission into a university in the Midwest region as an undergraduate who was 21 years old. The school culture, for Ngozi, was pretty much the same and similar with what she would have expected to find in a Nigerian university. Evelyn, on the other hand, experienced a culture shock concerning dress codes at the university where she studied in the Eastern part of Ohio. Evelyn explained that she grew up in a conservative Catholic family where her parents never let her wear dresses that revealed too much of her body. She also related that she arrived in the winter season and had no words to describe the shock she experienced about the frigid temperature. Okafor chimed in at this point to re-echo Evelyn's experience about the cold weather. He said the weather he met upon arrival almost made him quit and return to Nigeria. Then, he talked about the food, which made him to feel sick for many weeks because he was so used to African dishes. Therefore, the food culture constituted Okafor's culture shock.

Significant Themes

Following the codes and discussions on the concepts with the focus group, I developed three themes and discussed their relationship with the significant statements of the respondents. I created tables for each theme to portray how each code that constituted the theme relates with the responses of the participants. The questions or topics that warranted the participants' responses are included in the table. Below each table, I offered my views about what I thought the respondents were talking about and the possible ramifications of their views. A separate presentation of those two components ensured that the original data remained unadulterated. The following are the themes I developed, with indications of the relevant codes connected to them:

- *Self-actualization* (self-improvement; self-reliance; identity; social integration process)
- *Sense of the sacred* (moral values; charity-minded)
- *Communal spirit* (giving back; community development; solidarity; family ties; tribal sentiment; sense of entitlement).

Table 4.2.

Self-actualization

Codes	Questions/Topics	Participants' responses
Self-improvement	What was your purpose and aspirations coming into the United States?	Vin: "I came to study, have a career, and take care of myself. Viber: "I came to study to obtain a degree in business and go back." Freddick: "I arrived to study so that I could return to Nigeria and continue serving the government that sent me to the US." Winner: "We came to go to school." Haifa: "To integrate into the society, get a job and start contributing my own part to society."
Self-reliance	How integrating into the American society made you feel	Haifa: "I know my way around. I know how things work…there hasn't been much difficulty." Vin: "I liked the idea of being independent; it wasn't much of a big deal." Viber: "I adjusted very quickly and then integrated into the society."

		Freddick: "In about a month or two I got used to the American accents, you know… it didn't take me long to adapt." Winner: "They started understanding the stuff we were made of. Integration was so easy."
Identity	Social roles of NCC	Haifa: "Inculcate our history to the children so they don't get passive about their origin." To provide morale support in good and bad times. Vin: "We are all immigrants, in a very far away land. NCC should be like a home in a foreign place." Freddick: "My children here are more Americanized. I am trying to de-Americanize them to an extent to have Nigerian thing in them. I have only succeeded in doing it 5%."
Social integration	Experiences of social integration to the American society	Viber: "It was a shock in various ways, beginning with the weather. I wasn't used to the snow nor have I seen snow before… it was funny and given that I came here not having been to any higher institution in Nigeria. So, the instructional method was quite different from what I experienced in Nigeria before coming here." Freddick: "I have been reading magazines…and I was thinking every-

		where in America shooting, shooting, shooting everywhere, but when I came it wasn't so…. I realized that Americans are very very very friendly people. They say hi hi to people they know and people they don't know…. The only thing is that I had to get used to the way they speak their English, you know." Winner: "Really, before we came, we did kind of a research to know where we were gonna ask for admission. We knew at the time that at the Southern part of America you have more black people. We sought that place for admission really. We got admission at a Southern University… There really wasn't much difference because we all looked alike." Winner continued, "The only problem was, many of them at the time hadn't seen foreigners… When they see you, you look like them, but when you talk, they start asking, 'Where are you from'. Even in the classroom, 'Where are you from?' And a kind of, they start making fun of you the way you talk. That kind of thing is upsetting… In the classroom you weren't comfortable asking questions."

The responses from participants during the one-on-one interviews concerning their reasons for emigration generally pointed to Abraham Maslow's hierarchy of needs, the need for self-actualization, improvement, or determination (Maslow, 1970). In Maslow's pyramid of motivations, the need for self-actualization stood at the apex of the pyramid. It is the desire to attain one's potential and creative activities. Four out of the five participants that I interviewed pointed to this need as the purpose or the motivating force behind their decision to emigrate from Nigeria. Lack of educational opportunities, among other things, is one major cause of emigration. Quality education is no doubt a key to unlocking one's potentials, and four of the participants that I interviewed have doctorate degrees. In fact, one of them went back to school after his doctoral studies to obtain a Masters' degree in civil law. Three of the interviewees had returned to Nigeria following the completion of their studies but were forced to resettle back in the United States when things did not work out as they hoped.

Self-actualization and the determination to succeed in achieving it is the apparent driving force that seemed to help Nigerian immigrants through social integration process in a foreign land. Further discussions on this supposition with the focus group proved the assertion true. When faced with adaptation challenges, Ekene recalled how he had to serve as a waiter and later as a chef in a restaurant while completing his doctorate program. The identity issue and knowing where one came from is another factor that propels Nigerian immigrants to strive towards self-improvement. The stake is so high, with family and friends all having such a huge expectation from the person living in the diaspora. The person in the diaspora sees himself/herself as a means of sustenance and support for the people back home in Nigeria.

Table 4.3.

Sense of the Sacred

Preliminary codes	Questions/Topics	Participants' responses
Moral values/spiritual role	What roles would you like the NCC to play in your life?	Vin: In addition to the spiritual nourishment that NCC provides, it ought to give us a taste of home and not let us lose our values. Viber: Hopes for NCC to strengthen his faith and the community's faith that we may subscribe strongly to the teachings of Jesus Christ who taught that whatever you do unto the least of my brothers is what you do unto me. "So, there are orphanages, there are all kinds of things that we can do to help the poor masses back home." Freddick: "We need to have a little bit of home flavor in the community here… during time of happiness, the times of joy, or sadness, the Catholic Church is always there for us." The sense of belonging the NCC provides is a nice way for us to begin to see how we can help people in Nigeria. Winner: For the NCC to deepen her spiritual life and help to

		strengthen marriage and family life because divorce rate among Nigerians in the diaspora is very high.
Charity-minded	Do you give to charity?	Viber reflects on his poverty-stricken childhood and is grateful to God for the success he has achieved in life and as such feels obligated to give back to support others in his community in thanksgiving to God. Freddick: Most of Freddick's charity efforts are here in the USA and are faith-based or in thanksgiving to God for his health. He donates to the Kidney society because his father died of kidney-related problems. He donates to Cancer society because his cancer is in remission or has ceased. In addition, he donates to Faith Family Institute. Winner and her husband give out up to $20,000 annually to charity, both here in the USA and Nigeria. The plight of women, elderly people and children who are in need concerns her most. Haifa: "I still give to charity, I give to Church, I give to other charities... before I left the coun-

		try where I used to live and most of my things were given to St. Vincent de Paul, which is a Catholic charity organization." Vin donates to the Catholic Church and food pantries, but in addition, he helps people who cannot afford the professional fees of his work.

Each of the respondents in the Table 4.3 viewed spirituality as the basic role they expected the NCC as an organization to play in their lives. Viber hopes that the NCC would strengthen his faith and religious practices. Winner expects the NCC to help her and others in strengthening their bond of marriage and general family life. It appears that the motivation for rendering acts of charity is also connected to the people's faith in God. Freddick donates to charity in thanksgiving to God for his good health while Viber remembers his humble beginnings and donates to charity as a sign of gratitude to God.

There is a fundamental deference to the divine in the African culture, as religion seems to be the fulcrum around which every activity revolves in African societies (Idang, 2015). In the primitive African culture, the belief existed that deities owned the land and its people. Ekeke and Ekeopara (2010) argued in their research that in the traditional Africa there is no atheist[1]. Consequently, to transgress against one's neighbor is to incur the wrath of the gods. Similarly, to disrespect one's elder is to bring bad omen to one's future. All other ethos and cultural observances, like ancestral worship, religious reverence, moral etiquette, and so on, hinge on the African's sense of the sacred. Mbiti (1989) observed that

---

[1] The authors further exposed the notion of Supreme Being in the African traditional belief system and listed some attributes of God, which predates any Christian religious influence in Africa (pp. 209-213).

Africans are notoriously religious, and each African society has its own religious system. Indeed, a strong sense of religion permeates all the facets of life in the African traditional society, so much so that, it is not easy to isolate it (Mbiti, 1989). As such, there is that sense of the transcendental which pervades everything in the African worldview. Moreover, since traditional religion is so in-depth in all aspects of life, there is no formal distinction between the spiritual and the secular in the traditional African society (Mbiti, 1989).

Schein (1992) explained culture to be a pattern of shared basic assumptions that a group learned overtime as it solved problems of external adaptation and internal integration. This pattern of shared basic assumptions influences the perspectives and approaches to life events as the African interacts with the world. The initial "culture shock" that African immigrants often experienced upon arrival in a Western culture may not unrelated with the absence of a sense of the sacred or sense of religion in an industrialized society. There are no atheists in the traditional African societies because religion was always an integral and inseparable part of the entire culture, regulating one's entire action (Mbiti, 1989; Onwubiko, 1991). The African immigrant's integration process to a modern society is therefore reflective of the one's religious concepts and basic assumptions. Mbiti (1989) affirmed that one of the sources of severe strain for the African, when exposed to modern changes through emigration, education, or urbanization, is the increasing process of being detached from one's traditional environment. I will discuss further on the sense of the sacred concept in the next Chapter.

Table 4.4.

Communal Spirit

Giving back	What roles would you like the NCC to play in your life?	Vin: In addition to the spiritual nourishment that NCC provides, it ought to give us a taste of home and not let us lose our values. Viber: Hopes for NCC to strengthen his faith and the community's faith that we may subscribe strongly to the teachings of Jesus Christ who taught that whatever you do unto the least of my brothers is what you do unto me. "So, there are orphanages, there are all kinds of things that we can do to help the poor masses back home." Freddick: "We need to have a little bit of home flavor in the community here… during time of happiness, the times of joy, or sadness, the Catholic Church is always there for us." The sense of belonging the NCC provides is a nice way for us to begin to see how we can help people in Nigeria. Winner: For the NCC to deepen her spiritual life and help to strengthen marriage and family life because divorce rate among Nigerians in the diaspora is very high.
Community development	Opinions about community	Haifa: "There are a lot of things that our people need back there in Nigeria, most of their needs are not being met by the

	development	government. So we that are living in the diaspora we have to supplement those needs by being generous and contributing towards community development in different places. Maybe in education, health, or even general assistance with skills and training and business."
		Vin: "Many things that could be done at home where our government are not doing anything."
		Viber: I feel grateful to God for what I am today, and I feel I have to give back to the society."
		Freddick: "It's something worth doing, but we have to get the structures right first. You have to ensure that the gifts get to the intended people."
		Winner: "I volunteer in places here to do community development, example and foodbanks. In Nigeria, I assist women, elderly people, and children."
Solidarity	Supporting family and friends in Nigeria and the need for remittances and helping others	Haifa: "I think it's important to support family and friends, and this view of mine will not change anytime soon. As we are living in diaspora we have to supply the needs of the people back home."
		Vin: "Every now and then there is a death or something like that back home; we send them money to support."
		Viber: "Before I came here (for the interview), I got a phone call from home of

		some relative who needs to bury a family member and it involves money. I will give and I'm not going to write it down anywhere." Freddick: "ten percent of my earnings go to help family members back home. A death in the family means a big chunk of money to be contributed." Winner: "Constantly sending money home. Constantly… When we finish I will show you my receipt the one I sent yesterday… We give a lot, but I'm happy to do it."
Family ties	Maintaining relationship with family while living abroad	Haifa: "My relationship is still the same as before, very good, cordial. We are in constant contact. I speak to my family almost every day." Vin: "The only relative at home was mum and I had great relationship with her." Viber: "… I grew up in a strong Catholic environment…, so, we were in touch and have remained in touch." Freddick: "My relationship with them is okay, if only they'd stop being insatiable… thinking that a help from me is their birthright… Otherwise, my relationship with them is good." Winner: "Great relationship with family."

Tribal sentiment	Collective effort towards community development	Haifa: "I think we should not restrict ourselves to community development here (in the USA) because at the end of the day we are here but we have people over there in Nigeria who have needs." He acknowledged that it is true that when you go to Nigeria, we hail from various states. Moreover, even in those states there are people from different communities, making people to wonder, "where will the project be done?" Freddick is not concerned with the tribal sentiment but with the need to ensure that contributions get to the right people who need them. He thinks that the current structure of NCC is not sufficient to ensure this process. Vin recalled an experience he had with an Igbo Union he belonged to in the state you used to live. Although the Igbos are one tribe, yet, "… you have the Imo state man, the Anambra State man, the Abia state man, everybody bringing their own sense and all that, and things were just stalled." He concluded, "I think the Church will be a better institution or channel that can meticulously carry out these functions as opposed to lay folks that have all the political, tribal motives…" Viber: Collective effort is an ideal thing

		to do if and only if all of us agreed to make sacrifices…. We can do simple things such as helping to renovate primary schools or providing them with chairs and even toilet facilities… because if we help one, they will help the rest…" Winner: "It's great, but the problem I foresee in that one…, if I say let's do it, are you going to do it in Enugu, Anambra, or Imo?"
Sense of entitlement	Helping relatives and friends back home in Nigeria	Viber: Vin: "They bug you with phone calls for money… nobody calls you from home to ask how you are…. In general, they think that you pluck money from the trees." Freddick: "As soon as I got a job, it was like I should solve all their problems for them…" Winner: "… the only friendship is money. That's the connection…. If you don't send them money, they say you have forgotten them." Haifa: "I give to charity. Gave away all my belongings when I relocated to the US."

The responses given by participants as was shown in Table 4.4 portrayed the connection between various facets of the people's value system, spirituality, charity, family ties, tribe, togetherness, and community development. Though the respondents detest the constant demands for financial assistance from their folks in Nigeria, yet, they continually make remittances willy-nilly. Table. 4.4 laid out the responses of participants that summarily pointed to their underlying communal spirit. Haifa, for instance, regarded the support he renders to family and friends in Nigeria as an obligation, which he has no plans of stopping anytime soon. Winner affirmed that she is constantly sending money to family and friends back in Nigeria but that she is happy doing so. Such spirit of solidarity prompts the people in the diaspora to make remittances to their people and to support collective efforts toward community development.

Communalism is a principal offshoot from the basic assumptions of the African sense of religion. It is an autochthonous communal spirit that pervades traditional African societies (Onwubiko, 1991). Research found that traditional African societies are communal in nature (Achebe, 1958; Mbiti, 1989; Onwubiko, 1991). I formulated this theme from the expressions of participants that seemed to point towards tribal sentiment, sense of entitlement, the need to give back, and their continuous references to paucity of numbers in the NCC. All these were pointers to one major element of the African culture, the communal spirit. It is linked to the concept of "our people" as was discussed and validated in the focus group. This sense of communalism is observable in traditional African cultures and influences individual self-determination. As such, being in position to provide for and give assistance to others, to our people, influences the African's need to strive for success.

This type of spirit is synonymous with the deep sense of kinship identified as one of the strongest forces in traditional African life (Mbiti, 1989). Kinship controls social relationships among people in an African community, governing blood relations, regulating marital customs, and determining behavior of one individual towards another (Mbiti, 1989). In fact, it is kinship that binds and regulates the entire life of a given tribe and beyond, extending even to the departed and those yet to be born (Mbiti, 1989). The sacredness of life and preservation of the unborn, as well as ancestral worship in African traditional religion find their origins in the kinship system (Mbiti, 1989).

The African sense of communalism inevitably breeds tribal sentiment as the individuals who make up a village find ancestral affinity between them and by extension, an affinity between people of that tribe. This connection affects both the learned and the illiterate equally as was evident in the responses of participants in the one-on-one interviews concerning collective efforts toward community development. Nigerians in the diaspora hold fast to and maintain strong leaning toward their tribes of origin no matter how many years they have been away from home. This is not entirely a mere tribal perspective, because it is such sentiments that foster continued remittances from those living in the diaspora to the local folks. One of the interviewees, Haifa, maintained that he will never stop giving back to family and friends back home in Nigeria. Tribal sentiment gives identity to the African as he or she can only fully define himself or herself according the person's worldview.

Summary

This chapter presented results from the interviews and group discussions, generating compelling themes from the analysis of data. Findings from the chapter portrayed a quintessence African sense of solidarity, which relates to the African communal spirit. In the traditional African parlance, solidarity portrays an underlying assumption commonly understood among Africans to connote the community of brothers and sisters irrespective of consanguinity. An Igbo theory that connotes solidarity is Umunna-bụ-ike, whose loose English translation is kinship or kinsmanship. I will explain this theory in detail in Chapter V. Kinship refers to blood relations, but Umunna-bụ-ike goes beyond blood relation to refer to a deeper sense of solidarity that transcends consanguinity. It is a term that includes people that do not really have blood relationship who work together for a common goal. This type of unity of purpose is usually observed among migrant people in the diaspora as they rally together to seek better ways to improve the quality of life for their people back home. At this level, people shelve tribal sentiment for the greater good of pursuing common goals. It could be what leads them to form diaspora organizations. Sometimes this sense of solidarity conflicts with tribal sense and if not handled properly could lead to the disintegration of that group. Faith-based groups having underlying religious sentiments easily diffuse tribal sentiments and generate one strong sense of solidarity. The NCC is a faith-based organization that can utilize religious adherence to achieve such sense of solidarity and unity of purpose.

5

CONCLUSIONS AND DISCUSSIONS

The purpose of Chapter V is to apply the analyzed data described in the preceding chapter to my theoretical frameworks, to use the compelling themes that emerged from the analysis to answer the research questions, and finally relate them to the topic of my research. The chapter is in five sections. The first section relates research data to the theoretical frameworks of this research. The second section uses the compelling themes that emerged from data analysis to answer my three research questions. The third section uses an Igbo theory to present the implications of this study in the light of my research topic. The fourth section discusses suggestions for future research. Finally, the last section presents a conclusion to the research.

Relating Data to the Theoretical Frameworks

Lewin's Planned Change Model/Action Research

Kurt Lewin, who founded the Planned Change Model (PCM) for organizational development, was born of Jewish origin in a German village that was part of Poland (Levine & Hogg, 2010). Survival and the quest for self-actualization often engender migration, as was the case for Lewin who fled Nazi Germany in 1934 and immigrated to the United States amidst rampant discrimination that would later threaten the very existence of his Jewish community (Aman, 2014; Levine & Hogg, 2010). In the same way, albeit, prompted by a different theatre of war, one of the focus group members in my research shared her experiences about her escape from Nigeria during the 1967 – 1970 civil war. Lewin's experiences in an anti-Semitic society influenced his view about human behavior and drove his focus on group processes (Levine & Hogg, 2010). Thus, his Planned Change Model, evident in his Action Research, dominated his social psychology and led to further developments on group processes.

Similarly, Lewin's social environment influenced his development of field theory, a framework for understanding human behavior in relation to social environments of the individual (Levine & Hogg, 2010). Adelman (1993) observed that, by using democratic participation rather than autocratic coercion, Lewin demonstrated the greater gain in productivity. Lewin aimed at using this platform to promote social justice by trying to raise the self-esteem of minority groups in order to help them seek independence, equality, and co-operation (Adelman, 1993). Participants in the one-on one interview often referred to self-improvement or financial independence as their motivation for coming to the United States. Indeed, they were seeking to gain or regain self-esteem and equality in a new and advanced society.

Self-actualization, therefore, stands out as a fundamental drive among diaspora people. It is rooted in the people's quest for self-improvement, self-reliance, identity, and social integration. Lewin believed that social problems should be central to the concerns of psychologists, it should be central to policy makers in a diversity-rich society. A systematic study of a problem and their possible solutions helps in understanding the phenomenon (Levine & Hogg, 2010). This research attempted to systematically present the nature of a diaspora people and identify the basic drive in them, like self-actualization, in order to find solutions to the improvement of their organizations.

On another note, Lewin's action research was rooted in the principles of group dynamics where a spiral process of data collection, theorizing, and assessment bring about the desired change (Adelman, 1993). Lewin referred to these phases of change as unfreezing, moving, and refreezing (Adelman, 1993; Cummings & Worley, 2009; French & Bell, 1999). These change processes take place in a functional environment and become successful by carrying the people involved in the process along. As a participatory, democratic process, action research is simultaneously concerned with bringing about change in organizations, in self-improvement among organizational members, and adding to scientific knowledge (Coghlan & Brannick, 2014). Communal spirit relates to this participatory process, which creates the environment for the actualization of individual potentials.

Hartzell (2018) explained that unfreezing is the stage of creating the awareness about how the status quo is hindering the organization in some way. The awareness is necessary to forestall resistance to change and for encouraging participation in the change process. Lewin taught that old behaviors and past ways of thinking cause some natural resistance to change and communication is important at this stage, to keep people informed about the imminent change (Hartzell, 2018). People in the organization have to see how necessary a planned change is for the improvement of the organization to motivate their participation in the change process.

My research aimed at highlighting the pertinent need for organizational improvement of the Nigerian Catholic Chaplaincy in Central Ohio (NCC). Coghlan and Brannick (2014) opined that such effort is an evolving process undertaken in a spirit of collaboration and co-inquiry to engender organizational members' participation in the change process. Linking the Nigerian immigrants' desire for self-actualization to organizational improvement of NCC would motivate their participation towards common goals as a diaspora organization. Individuals in the organization have naturally striven for self-improvement and social integration, pulling together their drive in an intergroup relationship would bring about an organized action toward community development. This is because as Schein (1992) noted, cultural assumptions revolve around all aspects of a group's interaction with the external environment, such that, consensus plan of action is required if a group is to perform effectively.

The changing and moving stage in action research is the transitioning stage, which happens during the implementation stage of the change process. In Lewin's view, this is when the change becomes real because it is at this stage that people begin to learn the new behaviors, processes, and ways of thinking (Hartzell, 2018). At this stage, education, communication, and support are necessary to keep the people focused on the need for change and ultimately how the organization could benefit from it. Nigerians in the diaspora exhibit the communal spirit and the traditional sense of kinship (Mbiti, 1969), like other Africans in the diaspora. This sense of kinship engenders unity of purpose and the desire to contribute their resources for community development among the diaspora Nigerians. The suggested education and communication at the changing stage in Lewin's 3-stage change theory would further ensure that the members of NCC understand the benefit of their communal actions and motivate more collaboration in the organization.

When the organization is at its optimal state after making the necessary changes, Lewin opined that stabilizing and reinforcing this stage should be the objective of the organization (Hartzell, 2018). He described this stage as the freezing stage. Coghlan and Brannick (2014) referred to it as the stage for evaluating action, wherein, the organization evaluates both the intended and unintended outcomes of the applied changes. At this stage, solidifying and refreezing the organizational processes, goals, and new norms are necessary measures to ensure that people do not revert to their old ways of thinking and behaving (Hartzell, 2018).

The goal of this research was to find ways of improving the NCC as a faith-based organization so that it can collaborate better with other agencies toward community development. The unfreezing stage, as part of action research, is what this research is accomplishing by creating awareness of the status quo among participants of the one-on-one interviews and members of the focus group. The awareness prompted meaningful responses and might achieve the same effect when applied at the organizational level. Coghlan and Brannick (2014) referred to it as the stage of planning action, exploring and constructing the context and purpose of the project. This dovetails into the moving stage where implementation and transitioning occur until the process arrives at the evaluation stage. Concerning the freezing stage, Lewin emphasized on making efforts to see that the changes made are not lost but cemented into the organization's culture to become the accepted way of thinking and doing things (Hartzell, 2018). This does not mean closing the opportunities for further growth, but solidifying an implemented change prepares the organization for future improvements while ensuring that there is no relapse back to the old ways of thinking and doing things.

Social Transformation Theory

Social transformation implies a fundamental change in society, encompassing a wide range of institutional and cultural changes that occur in the society throughout history; especially when two cultures meet and integrate varying elements of each culture with the other (Castles, 2010; Khondker & Schuerkens, 2014). Social Transformation Theory (STT) developed from several studies on ancient societies and the social impacts of migration and social integration of migrants in the host society. Tinajero and Sinatti (2011) studied a bottom-up approach to migration for development, seeking to find how migration could contribute effectively to development. The authors found that achievement of meaningful improvement could be possible by viewing migration and development through the lens of human development, involving organizations at local and grassroots' levels as well as engaging diaspora organizations in social development strategies (Tinajero, & Sinatti, 2011).

Again, social transformation is a theory based on the premise that social changes occur between the poles of diversity and integration (Khondker & Schuerkerns, 2014). Khondker and Schuerkerns (2014) explained that integration is the degree of probability of a change of characteristics of a specific system, while diversity as a system's structure deduce from the distribution of characteristics of a system's elements. The authors concluded that social development or transformation is a process that links the levels of integration and diversity where the growth of these levels means the direction of social development. When the system has attained its limits of diversity and integration transformation occurs and a new principle of integration of a society appears, representing a transformation of the system and its characteristic structures (Khondker & Schuerkerns, 2014). The social patterns and transformation following the French system of colonization is an example, wherein, decades of colonization of African nations by France did not obliterate certain cultural elements of the African groups, which perdured and interacted with Western cultural elements, giving rise to social transformation in both France and the colonized nations (Khondker & Schuerkerns, 2014). The three themes that emerged from my research (self-actualization, sense of the sacred, and communal spirit), are vestiges of African cultural elements which members of the NCC and other African immigrants exude in their host society and which could evoke social transformation.

Therefore, understanding cultural assumptions and possible contributions of migrants to the host society could be key to more positive social transformation (Castles, 2010). De Haas (2010) supported this idea in his concept of migrant networks as a form of social capital. The author opined that since social capital is an aggregate of the actual or potential resources in the institutionalized relationships of mutual acquaintance between the migrant and the host society, these resources and their connected networks amount to significant social capital in a given society. Castles (2010) agreed that the conceptual framework of migration studies encapsulates the true understanding of modern societies. Migrants also needed to, introspectively familiarize themselves with knowledge of their own ethnology for a positive identity and effective contribution to social transformation. In the case of diaspora Nigerians, for instance, awareness of their culturally motivated self-actualization, sense of the sacred, and spirit of communalism would help in the organizational improvement of the NCC. Improved performance of the NCC would facilitate collaboration and participation with local communities in the USA as well as Nigeria toward development efforts. The resources and knowledge that migrants gather in the diaspora foster human and economic development in their origin societies and in their host countries (Castles, 2010; Castles et al., 2013; de Haas, 2010).

The themes from this study are, in a way, representative of the worldview of the participants who are Nigerian-born African immigrants. The traditional African world is a world of animate, inanimate, and spiritual beings, interacting with the living in some sort of mystical association (Onwubiko, 1991). Evidence Sense of the sacred or sense of religion is in the fact that one's entire action in the traditional African society is reflective of one's religious concepts and practices (Onwubiko, 1991). One of the participants in the research's one-on-one interview, Viber, opined that organizational growth and increased participation would happen in the NCC when members pay attention to the words of Jesus Christ in the sacred scriptures. There is a deep connection between the sense of the sacred and sacredness of life, such that Africans uphold as sacred the sources of life (Onwubiko, 1991). By extension, humanitarian care is an integral and inseparable part of the African culture.

Therefore, when the African immigrates to a foreign country, the moral obligation to provide life sustenance for family and friends is one that arises from both the African sense of religion and sense of the sacredness of life. Castles and Miller (2009) affirmed that Africans abroad, whether refugees or economic migrants, high-income or low-income earners, send money to their families. The authors noted that remittances provide a crucial means of livelihood to millions of people, accounting for US$10.8 billion in remittance flow to Africa in 2007, according to the World Bank (Castles & Miller, 2009). This overarching need to send money home pushes the African immigrant to strive for self-actualization and good employment. The effect on the host society is a gradual increase in healthy competition toward educational and financial success (Gsir & Mescoli, 2015).

Furthermore, the concept of 'our people,' as was validated in one of the focus group meetings, is an underlying reason for emigration from African societies. The burning desire to help others (seen in the volume of remittances) and to build and develop communities at their societies of origin is a common feature among African immigrants. Thus, the searches for greener pastures and for self-actualization are usually not for self-serving purposes. Participants in the one-on-one interviews who are Nigerian immigrants revealed that they arrived in the United States seeking to improve themselves educationally and financially, but the purpose for the attainment of such positions was to assist others and to develop their local communities. African spirit of communalism is the basis for remittances and charity-minded actions of the African immigrants, which is deeply rooted in the traditional African's sense of religion and kinship. Research has shown that this sense of kinship and community lead to chain migration where prospective migrants learn of opportunities and are provided transportation and initial accommodation through their links with previous migrants (de Haas, 2010). The sense of kinship and community, as such, is not akin to only African immigrants but has been the phenomenon of migration networks (de Haas, 2010).

Participants in the one-on-one interviews continuously hinted at paucity of numbers in the NCC events. They all expressed their dismay at the low turnout of members for the Nigerian community ceremonies. Their sentiments mirror a deeper yearning for kinship, communality, and solidarity. Social transformation is about diversity and integration, which creates the possibility of a new element in the cycle of social change (Khondker & Schuerkens, 2014). Is it possible that the cultural diversity created by the social integration of African immigrants could bring about the creation of new elements in the United States' socio-cultural milieu? Apparently, it has influenced the diaspora Nigerians, and with proper restructuring, could influence the organizational structure of the NCC. Schein (1992) agreed that cultural assumptions evolve around all aspects of an organization's relationship with its external environment. The organizational improvement of NCC must be mindful of the basic underlying assumptions of the people, the espoused values, and the visible organizational structures and processes (Schein, 1992).

The emerging link between the theoretical frameworks of this study reflects in the common notion of viewing organizational change as an evolving phenomenon that requires a double-loop learning for productive participation of members. Argyris (1976) found that participants in organizations that encourage double-loop learning could question the fundamental design, goals, and activities of their organizations. This creates an environment where individuals can confront one another's views, leading to their arriving at the most valid information, to which participants can become internally committed because it came from their free and informed choices (Argyris, 1976). The application of Lewin's action research to organizational development usually starts with conducting brainstorming exercises with the team in order to question the status quo (Duggan, 2018). Thereafter, the organizations would ensure the management of the new changes and analysis of its outcome for a possible repetition of the process or stabilization of the new status quo. This is what double-loop model proffers as well.

In the same vein, the theoretical frameworks of this research promote the double-loop model in the sense of the collaborative ideologies they proffer. Kurt Lewin acknowledged that spirit of collaboration and co-inquiry are necessary tools for organizational improvement, to engender organizational members' participation in the change process (Coghlan & Brannick, 2014). Similarly, proponents of the Social Transformation Theory advocated for social development as a process that links the levels of integration and diversity where the growth of these levels determines the direction of social development (Khondker & Schuerkerns, 2014).

Relating the Three Themes to the Research Questions

The purpose of this section is to use the themes from research data to answer the three research questions and to relate them to the topic of this research. The overarching themes were, self-actualization, sense of the sacred, and communal spirit. These themes represented a summary of what the respondents said during the interviews and the meanings drawn from discussions with the focus group during data analysis process. These responses and sense making prompted the interview protocol, developed from the three research questions.

Self-actualization versus RQ 1: In what ways can one improve NCC organizationally, as a diaspora FBO, for more proactive roles in homeland community development?

Self-actualization and contribution to homeland development are some of the underlying elements that prompt people to migrate from their societies of origin to new ones (de Haas, 2010; Tinajero & Sinatti, 2011). The need to improve one's education or financial abilities motivated participants in the one-on-one interviews to search for greener pastures. NCC as a diaspora FBO, consists of people who arrived in the USA for self-improvement, academic pursuit, financial independence, and indeed, self-actualization. Haifa, one of the participants in the interview, opined that it is only when NCC as an organization has helped members to fulfill their quest for coming to the United States that unified efforts to help others back in Nigeria could be achieved.

In the same vein, research found that enlargement of people's capabilities, that is, what they were able to do and be in life, is the panacea to development (Tinajero & Sinatti, 2011). The authors concluded that the goals and means to development are the enhancement of people's intrinsic capacities like, knowledge, health, and self-respect, which make them capable of shaping their own destiny (Tinajero & Sinatti, 2011). This view agrees with self-actualization and the suggestion made by Haifa that to achieve any meaningful progress in collective efforts toward community development NCC must help its members to realize their dreams of immigrating to the United States. Studies show that migration and development have reciprocal relationship as migrants and the broader structure in which they live influence changes in each other (Aman, 2014; de Haas, 2010; Khondker & Schuerkerns, 2014; Tinajero & Sinatti, 2011). Aman (2014) found that different organizations like, hometown, ethnic, alumni, religious associations, NGOs, investment groups and even schools, are playing significant roles in connecting the diaspora to Africa's development. The bottom-up approach is how these small-scale actors can contribute more effectively in the development of both their host societies and their countries of origin (Tinajero & Sinatti, 2011). At the end of the day, people are the architects of their own development and assisting them to actualize their individual potentials will positively affect development.

Furthermore, organizational growth begins with personnel training and changes in organizational culture (Schein, 1992; Thompson, 2008). Assisting NCC members in their social integration process and supporting the education of their children would be a long-term answer to organizational improvement of the NCC. Responses from participants in the interview revealed that majority of Nigerian migrants who arrived in the 1980s came to improve themselves academically. This group of migrants constitute the first-generation diaspora Nigerians in the United States. Many of them achieved their educational goals and became economically independent and capable of engaging in diaspora efforts toward development. It behooves the NCC to ensure that its members continue to gain access to education and other opportunities for human development so to engage more effectively in various community development efforts, including partnership with governments and mainstream agencies for community development in the USA as well as in Nigeria.

Diaspora networking and information sharing will help the NCC to collaborate with other diaspora groups, having devised means of enhancing its members' capacities. Migrant networks form rich social capital that ought to be harnessed for community development (Aman, 2014; de Haas, 2010; Khondker & Schuerkerns, 2014). Study observed that the volume of social capital possessed by a person depends on the size of his or her network connections, and the volume of economic or cultural social capital possessed by each of those to whom he or she is connected (de Haas, 2010). This is part of the way diversity and integration bring about social transformation, which is why it is necessary to make efforts to ensure that different diaspora groups or migrant networks strive towards common objectives (Khondker & Schuerkerns, 2014; Tinajero & Sinatti, 2011).

Sense of the sacred versus RQ 2: How can NCC continue to fulfill the spiritual needs of members and still play major roles in social services delivery?

The traditional African sense of the sacred or religion informs the entire worldview of Africans (Mbiti, 1989; Onwubiko, 1991). The belief system and moral etiquette of the Africans revolve around that deep awareness of a supernatural order. Participants in the one-on-one interviews referred to the spiritual role that NCC needed to play in their lives. The one participant who did not see the need for this role said he was already gaining the spiritual aid from his parish church. Nevertheless, the Nigerian immigrants' sense of religion is pivotal to their charity-mindedness. In their review of faith-based organizations as social service providers, Bielefeld and Cleveland (2013b) found that religious motivation was consistent for volunteering because religion attracts, motivates, and sustains volunteers in Faith-based Organizations' (FBOs) social services delivery. Thus, ensuring that the spiritual life of the NCC is thriving would promote participation in humanitarian acts and other social services delivery. Research findings agreed that religious involvement, community attachment, and socioeconomic status were main predictors for who is most likely to volunteer or donate towards the community's social service delivery (Bielefeld & Cleveland, 2013b).

Indeed, there is a Center for Interfaith Action on Global Poverty (CIFA), whose objective is to serve as a bridge between FBOs and secular development communities (Duff, 2010). This interfaith organization gives voice to the capacities of the faith sector and advocates for their full engagement with governments, Non-governmental Organizations (NGOs), other mainstream agencies, and private philanthropy, in their global effort to eradicate poverty and diseases (Duff, 2010). The NCC upholds similar objectives as CIFA and can do more as a migrants' organization through networking with other diaspora organizations and collaborating with groups like CIFA, for greater impact on social services delivery. Bielefeld and Cleveland (2013b) concluded that religion attracts and motivates volunteers to support the social works of FBOs. Likewise, spiritual exercises and other community activities at the NCC enhance the diaspora Nigerians' sense of religion, which in turn sustains the desire to volunteer and to donate towards social services objectives among members.

Communal spirit versus RQ 3: How can the diaspora NCC attain better organizational structure to collaborate more with other NGOs in social services delivery towards homeland community development?

NCC is a diaspora organization that consists of members of the same faith adherence. Sense of community is expectedly a constitutive element of any Christian group as the Lord Jesus Christ in John 17:13, "... that they may be one." The Christian principle of love for neighbor and the double-loop model of allowing members to brainstorm together in the organization's affairs would lead to internal commitment and better organized NCC. Collaboration with other diaspora groups and NGOs can only be effective when the internal organization of the NCC is viable and efficient.

Communal spirit, which was the fulcrum on which traditional African societies revolved, is a compelling theme in this research. Tribal sentiment, kinship, and sense of solidarity exhibited by diaspora Nigerians, as were observed in the data analysis, emanate from their sense of communalism. Mbiti (1989) noted that the word, family, has a much wider circle of members than what it connotes in Europe or North America. It is like a vast network that stretches horizontally, relating everybody to everybody (Mbiti, 1989). In Africa, family hood is so expansive that each person is a brother or sister, father or mother, grandmother or grandfather, or cousin, or brother-in-law, or uncle or aunt, to everybody else (Mbiti, 1989, Onwubiko, 1991). This versatile kinship system extends to include the departed, believed to be always present, and the unborn (Mbiti, 1989). Industrialization and urbanization seem to have destroyed this network of kinship system, but it really has given it a broader spectrum, because, individuals from the same town now regard each other as brothers or sisters when outside of their town. It is this sense of communalism that operates among diaspora Nigerians who, by extension, regard each other as relatives while far away from country of origin.

The spirit of communalism continues to exist wherever Africans find themselves. Onwubiko (1991) concluded that the community is the custodian of the individual because the African is known and identified in, by, and through his community. Organization of the NCC for better collaboration with other mainstream agencies should include the encouragement of this communal spirit and the inculcation of it to second-generation diaspora Nigerians. Aman (2014) included identity building and awareness raising as part of the activities developmental organizations should be engaging in for fuller participation of diaspora and mainstream organizations toward community development. In addition, as an embodiment of unique social capitals, NCC can collaborate more effectively with NGOs and other interest groups in community development, by creating common goals between them and the groups. De Haas (2010) defined migrant networks as social ties based on kinship, friendship, and community membership that connects migrants, former migrants, and non-migrants in origin and destination countries. The African sense of community has a strong role to play in using migrant networks to facilitate better collaboration between NCC and other NGOs toward social services delivery in their areas of residence as well as for homeland development.

Relating the Themes to the Research Topic

The three overarching themes from research data relate to a tripartite classification of the research topic thus:

- Organizational improvement – Self-actualization
- Faith-based organization – Sense of the sacred or religion
- Partnership for community development – Spirit of communalism

Linking these themes to unique aspects of my topic was an inspiration that came to me while on retreat at a monastery in Kentucky. I came to realize that the significant statements of participants and my focus group were all the time speaking to the various aspects of my research topic. This was my 'aha' moment during the data analysis phase of my research. The entire topic took on an altogether newer sense and my fulfillment at discovering the link between my topic and the responses of participants in the research was incomparable.

Organizational improvement – Self-actualization

Organizations influence the individuals in it just as the individuals affect changes in the organization (Thompson, 2008). Our organizational experiences shape us and define who we are because, in the end, our choice of occupation influences our quality of life (Thompson, 2008). Organizational improvement that hopes to succeed focuses on the development of its professional capital. Hargreaves and Fullan (2012) defined professional capital as the long-term investment in human, social, and decisional capital development with a view of reaping the rewards of economic productivity and social cohesion in the next generation. Although the authors based their arguments on educational development through the grooming and retention of high-quality teachers, their theory is applicable in organizational life generally because any organization seeking to grow would want to invest in developing its human capital (Hargreaves & Fullan, 2012).

Thus, self-development, which begins from early childhood, finds significant improvement and actualization in later adulthood within organizational life. Responses from participants in the one-on-one interviews indicated that self-improvement and ultimately, self-actualization inform the African immigrants' quest for immigration. The inner drive for self-actualization propels the overarching drive to seek better life, which is the motivation for migration. Castles and Miller (2009) observed that movement of people across borders have shaped states and societies reaching up to a global level and these have enormous economic and social consequences. Therefore, as organizational experiences shape individuals within it and the individuals in turn shape the organization, so does migration affect host societies while the society affect them (Castles, 2010; Castles & Miller, 2009; Khondker & Schuerkems, 2014; Thompson, 2008). The African immigrants go through the phases of integration and adaptation in a foreign culture. This process radically transforms them just as the change process also affects the host society over time.

Faith-based organization – Sense of the sacred or religion

Life in the primitive African society revolved around a deep sense of the divine, where the traditional African religion was the formative element of African thought, influencing the African culture itself (Onwubiko, 1991). African traditional religions have no creeds to recite, instead, the creeds are written in people's hearts and each person is a living creed of the tribe's religion (Mbiti, 1989). Ancestor worship, respect for life, communal spirit, moral codes, and social codes of conduct are offshoots from the traditional African sense of the divine. It is no wonder that the Nigerian chaplaincy as a faith-based organization is of great importance to the Nigerian Catholics in the diaspora. One of the interviewees reasoned that, "...if Christ sacrificed himself for the atonement of our sins ... why can't we make monetary sacrifice or any effort that we can to help the impoverished communities back home in Nigeria?" (Viber). This participant revealed the interconnectedness of his charity-driven spirit to his sense of religion. Although it is about his Christian beliefs, yet, the connection is out of the deep African sense of religion.

Moreover, research found that there is no unanimity of beliefs and practices in the African traditional religion because, the sense of religion is in the whole system of the African; he is simply a religious being (Mbiti, 1989). This may not be peculiar to only the traditional African societies, but I am interested in presenting this identifiable characteristic here as a formative element of the African culture. The reason is that it is an underlying lens or set of assumptions from which the African interacts with the external world. Sense of the sacred or religion plays pivotal role in the African immigrant's social integration process and safeguards his or her identity as he or she explores the new society in the diaspora. In the discussion about promoting collective efforts toward development, the focus group suggested that, the more retreats and community programs the NCC organizes, the more people would overcome those little things that create division among people thus solidifying communal spirit. This reflects the African's sense making process and the connection religion has with everything including community development. The more prayerful and spiritual people are in union with one another the easier it would be to act with a common sense of purpose.

Partnership for community development – Spirit of communalism

Communal spirit as an offshoot from the sense of the sacred ensures that the African immigrant retains his or her identity and maintains a continued link with his or her country of origin. This ideation influences the immigrant's continued remittances and promotes the zeal for community development among the diaspora people. The story of Viber who could not obtain a doctorate degree due to work schedules, yet, happily sponsored the education of his nephew back in Nigeria to obtain doctorate degree, is a good example of the African person's spirit of kinship. Viber was contented with his nephew's achievement because he felt like the success of his nephew is a communal gain for the family. This spirit of communalism provides fertile ground for promoting partnerships between the diaspora communities and other parties that are interested in community development.

Aman (2014) found that the sense of communalism is an essential element of migration networks, which helps to create viable partnerships for enhancing positive development. Study encouraged the promotion of tangible partnerships between governments, diaspora development practitioners, and mainstream development agencies (Aman, 2014). Similarly, partnerships between diaspora organizations like the NCC and agencies that are interested in the economic growth of underdeveloped countries enhances the role of diaspora organizations while fostering the spirit of communalism or togetherness (Aman, 2014; Tinajero, & Sinatti, 2011). Data from my research indicated that participants strongly supported the idea of collective efforts and strategic partnerships with agencies for community development. The African sense of communalism makes the initiation of this strategy possible and promising.

Umunna-bụ-ike theory and the research topic

A synonymous description of the Igbo word, Umunna-bụ-ike, is Strength in Kinship or Kinsmanship. Dictionary definition of kinsman in the less gender-sensitive era may render it as a blood relative, usually male, because there is also kinswoman. It defined kinsman as a blood relative, a relative by marriage, or a person of the same nationality or ethnic group (Dictionary.com, 2018). Kinsman usually appears in both a narrow and larger sense and the larger sense of its use relates to the theory of Umunna-bụ-ike in this research. The larger sense of the word, kinsmanship is,

A bond shared between two or more individuals. It's more than friendship; it's more than love itself. There is closeness, a sense of fierce loyalty to someone not of blood relation. Kinsmanship takes time to be forged; there is a sense of shared trust and honor. Most often it's unspoken. Kinsmanship in its nature is in no way to be taken lightly (Urban dictionary, 2016).

My personal observations of members of the NCC showed how the members assisted their relations, nephews, nieces, cousins, and in-laws. The assistance extends sometimes to friends or distant relatives from the same town. At the house of one of the interview participants, a young man of about 24 years old was there when I visited. When I asked who the new face was, I found out he was from their village and had just arrived from Nigeria, hoping to get his immigration papers sorted out in order to find a job. This young man has no consanguinity with the host family as I learned. In the same vein, another member of our NCC had returned from Nigeria with a 12 years old son of his late brother. When I asked what plans he had for the boy, he explained that he has adopted the young man so that he might gain the opportunity to succeed in life here in the United States. Kinsmanship is indeed alive and strong in diaspora communities.

In Umunna-bụ-ike theory is embedded, the Africans' sense of the sacred, the striving for self-actualization, communal spirit, the desire for numerical strength, and other organizational development concepts. The topic of my dissertation encapsulates and addresses these themes. The organizational improvement of a diaspora FBO consisting of African immigrants proposes to use this theory in finding strategic partnerships for increasing rural and community development in the country of origin. The community's sense of the sacred is the operating force that draws the diaspora people into a community while fostering the selfless element of self-actualization for collective efforts toward community development. Mbiti (1989) opined that belief system generally motivates what people do, and what they believe springs from what they experience. Therefore, belief influences action in African traditional society just like the culture of an organization influences organizational outcomes (Mbiti, 1989; Schein, 1992). The two components belong to a single whole.

Furthermore, Umunna-bụ-ike relates to the philosophy of Ujamaa, a Swahili word, signifying family hood, goodwill, or togetherness (Nyerere, 1987). Ujamaa asserts that a person becomes a person through the people or community. Julius Nyerere, an African leader and the first president of Tanzania, made the concept popular by using Ujamaa as a political-economic management model that promoted his national development project (Nyerere, 1987; Pratt, 1999). Kindanka (2016) reported that Nyerere built a nation from the scratch, always advocating the equality of Tanzanians and all people. He published a development blueprint that was based on African communal spirit or the spirit of 'others', bringing family units together, and fostering cohesion, love, and service (McHenry, 1980; Pratt, 1999). Nyerere generally advocated that African traditions should serve as the basis for all future African development (Nyerere, 1987; Onwubiko, 1991). The Roman Catholic Church posthumously declared him Servant of God for his continued encouragement of good neighborliness among Tanzanians (Kindanka, 2016). Servant of God is a recognition given to a person the Church identifies as heroic in virtue during his lifetime. It is also a preliminary step towards canonization as a saint in the Catholic Church (Kindanka, 2016).

Because data from the interviews led to the three compelling themes of self-determination, sense of the sacred, and communal spirit, the theory of Umunna-bụ-ike is a conceptual crowning of these themes. Just as Julius Nyerere applied the concept of Ujamaa to a national development project, the concept of Umunna-bụ-ike could be used in the organizational development of NCC towards strategic partnership for rural and community development. Umunna bụ ike relates to communal spirit, and by extension, to authentic Christian spirit. Indeed, positive organizational development values; double-loop model, action research, transformational leadership, and so on, are identifiable with the theory of Umunna-bụ-ike. The theory brings out the power of unity, as the team is always stronger than the single person is (Thompson, 2008).

Umunna-bụ-ike also relates to Mary Parker Follett's concept of organizational synergy, explained in Eylon (1998)'s article on understanding empowerment. Follett strongly "believed that only through group activity could the full potential of individuals be realized (Eylon, 1998, p.19). The notion of synergy within the context of an organization came from the fact that an organization is more than the sum of its parts (Eylon, 1998; Thompson, 2008). As individuals interact and react in the organization, the relationship created becomes an entity in and of itself, which in turn triggers additional reactions. The relationship so created is more than the interacting individuals, whose actions has ripple effects on the organization, thus creating organizational synergy (Eylon, 1998). As a result, research observed that organizations are increasingly embracing horizontal cooperation as means of achieving excellence, passion, and involvement from employees (Eylon, 1998). Similarly, the notion of Umunna-bụ-ike promotes unity of purpose in the organization and among diaspora organizations. Members of the NCC could arrive at an organizational synergy through horizontal cooperation within the organization and in collaboration with other organizations interested in community development.

Suggestions for Future Research

This research bespeaks the need for comparative studies on diaspora organizations of African descent, to see how compelling themes from the study operate in the various ethnic groups and diaspora organizations. A study of such magnitude can be longitudinal or limited in scope, depending on research need and time availability. It can focus on Catholic chaplaincies in the diaspora or include all other diaspora faith-based organizations, but the constant ought to be their African origins. Such research would fulfill the concepts of Action Research as Lewin proposed, and could provide significant data to policy makers toward productive diversity and integration processes.

Consequently, this study challenges the course content of diversity training programs currently in use at various organizations. It questions how much background knowledge about the various cultures are included in these diversity and inclusion training modules? For example, understanding what "our people" signifies for Africans helps to understand the African's approach to interpersonal relationships. Incorporating the

African autochthonous spirit of kinship into organizational policies would influence how people interact and relate with each other in organizational settings. The double-loop learning and organizational synergy are both possible when the spirit of kinship pervades the organization. The term that is synonymous to kinship is camaraderie, which is mutual trust and friendship among people who spend quality time together. People usually spend 8 – 16 hours a day in their work environment. Kinship culture ensures camaraderie and can be pivotal to organizational success. It makes the case for the need to include it as a component in the curriculum for diversity and inclusion trainings.

On another note, governments and mainstream agencies can mirror diaspora remittance activities in becoming part of development efforts for poverty reduction and provision of healthcare for poorer communities. However, because Aman (2014) identified diaspora organizations as strategic agents of development, diaspora communities like the NCC needed to transcend from individual remittances to being organized and strategic agents of rural and community development. Yet, this level of functionality requires higher level of organization. Government policies and contributions of mainstream agencies of development can assist in this regard. They can organize seminars and awareness programs to support diaspora organizations in their efforts to maintain their identities and cultural values, such that new policies and plans are developed and implemented based on who they are as a people.

The United States Catholic Conference of Bishops (USCCB) recently increased interests in ethnic ministries and forming associations to study better ways of integrating different ethnic groups into the life of the Catholic Church in the United States. This research could serve as a motivation and a template of sorts for more ethnographic research on various ethnic groups in the Catholic Church here in the United States. Faith-based organizations can follow this pattern to increase integration processes that would have greater impacts on society.

Finally, studies have found that the resources and knowledge that migrants gather in the diaspora foster human and economic development in their origin societies and in their host countries (Castles, 2010; Castles et al., 2013; de Haas, 2010). Future research should seek to find ways to safeguard migrant groups from losing their identity, which indeed is part of their contribution to social transformation process. Diaspora Nigerians, for instance, should retain basic drives such as, self-actualization, sense of the sacred, and spirit of communalism, which are culturally motivated. Findings from such research would facilitate diaspora organizations' collaboration with governments and NGOs toward development projects.

Summary

Although my research topic centered on bringing rural and community development to Nigeria, this study found that migrant networks inevitably influence community development in societies where they reside as well. Khondker and Schuerkerns (2014) concluded that diversity and integration lead to social transformation while the interconnections of migrant networks influence the host society at different levels. As such, migration commissions ought to keep in mind the inevitable transformation the society undergoes through diversity and integration. Castles et al. (2013) concurred that, "While movements of people across borders have shaped states and societies since time immemorial, their global scope in recent years, their impact on domestic and international politics, as well as their enormous economic and social consequences have become distinctive" (p. 3). These authors envisioned that migration processes might become so entrenched and resistant to governmental control that new political forms may emerge. This is akin to the social transformation concept that Khondker and Schuerkerns (2014) discussed in their research, a radical transformation that affects all sphere of the society, changing the culture and the people. This concept also relates to the way organizations influence the individuals in it while the individuals affect changes in the organization (Thompson, 2008). Therefore, it is necessary to conduct comprehensive research on the various migrant cultures in the United States to assist the diversity and integration processes for positive social transformation outcomes.

On the other hand, diaspora communities, like the NCC must keep on upholding their autochthonous belief systems and incorporate them into their organizational culture. These belief systems, which evoke the spirit of communalism and inspire individuals toward self-actualization, are deep-rooted in the African sense of religion. Mbiti (1989) explained the belief system thus:

Traditional religions are not primarily for the individual, but for his community of which he is part. Chapters of African religions are written everywhere in the life of the community, and in traditional society there are no irreligious people. To be human is to belong to the whole community, and to do so involve participating in the beliefs, ceremonies, rituals and festivals of that community. A person cannot detach himself from the religion of his group, for to do so is to be severed from his roots, his foundation, his context of security, his kinship, and the entire group of those who make him aware of his own existence. To be without one of those corporate elements of life is to be out of the whole picture. Therefore, to be without religion amounts to a self-excommunication from the entire life of society, and African peoples do not know how to exist without religion. (p. 2)

Therefore, a successful integration for the African immigrant needed to include a welcoming religious environment. A description of an African immigrant's initial culture shock upon arrival in the Western society often includes the culture shock at the dearth of religious obeisance, or simply absence of sense of the sacred. Indeed, communal spirit in its pure practice leaves no one behind as everyone is looking out for the good of the other. Participants in the interview opined that the NCC must first assist members to achieve their goals in order to enhance collective effort towards community development. This is the way of the Africans, the Umunna-bụ-ike theory, working together towards common goals and achieving organizational synergy.

Suggested Action Steps for Organizational Improvement of the NCC

The research goal was to propose best practices for the NCC that would affect organizational changes toward meaningful contributions to community development while maintaining the organization's faith-based orientation. To accomplish the organizational improvement of a diaspora group, this research focused on those enshrined values of an ethnic community as a necessary step for deeper understanding of its culture. The research questions that guided the study included:

- RQ 1: In what ways can one improve NCC organizationally, as a diaspora FBO, for more proactive roles in homeland community development?
- RQ 2: How can NCC continue to fulfill the spiritual needs of members and still play major roles in social services delivery?
- RQ 3: How can the diaspora NCC attain better organizational structure to collaborate more with other NGOs in social services delivery towards homeland community development.

These are the informed action steps based on research findings from this dissertation:

- Organizational Restructuring of the NCC
- Promotion of the People's Enshrined Values
- Faith-sharing for Growth in Spiritual Life
- Practical Charity and Delivery of Social Services
- Quarterly Meetings to Review Feedbacks

Organizational Restructuring of the NCC

Restructuring is the act of reorganizing the operational or other structures of an organization for the purposes of improving performance and making the organization better positioned to address its current needs (De Lange, 2016). The NCC requires restructuring in order to meet its present need of better collaboration with mainstream agencies for community development. Research findings revealed that it is not just about the development needs in Nigeria, but the NCC can engage in community development efforts in the United States as well. Building partnership with other agencies for social services delivery here in the United States could become the springboard for future engagement in social services delivery outside the United States.

NCC can start by creating special committees or self-governing teams, to be in charge of various facets of the organization's life. Self-governing teams are unlike manager-led teams. Thompson (2008) opined that a self-governing team is a better choice in the organizational context because it provides the greatest potential in terms of commitment and participation. Manager-led teams operate based on the ideology that a manager can run things more effectively than a team can (Thompson, 2008). The chaplain functions as manager in the NCC context, but this could be the reason commitment and participation is lacking in the organization. Teams like, Project Team, Children and Youth Development Team, Faith-sharing Team, and Cultural Team are possible suggestions for the NCC. These self-governing teams could decide how to execute tasks, manage processes and monitor progress based on goals laid out by the organization. The executive board of the NCC could keep functioning as the oversight team that would identify needs and set up achievable organizational goals based on the identified needs.

Promotion of the People's Enshrined Values

The enshrined values, epitomized in this research by the theory of Umunna-bu-ike, is at the core of organizational improvement. The theory embodies kinship, equality, fairness, and justice. Much of what hinders organizational growth revolve around the management of staff. If there is so much as a perceived unfair treatment among the staff, its overall effect negatively affects productivity in the long term. Cultivating the organizational culture of kinship would promote unity of purpose in an organization and tremendously improve organizational outcomes.

Faith-sharing for Growth in Spiritual Life

NCC as a faith-based organization ought to develop continuous faith-sharing programs where members could gather for sharing life experiences in the journey of faith. The identity of an FBO is tied to its spirituality, which finds expression in the charity works of such an organization. It is paramount to the maintenance of its identity that a FBO should continue to renew its spiritual life.

Embarking on the provision of social services could easily distract the core values of NCC. Care must be taken to ensure that faith-sharing and other spiritual exercises are regularly organized for members to maintain the spiritual aspect of the organization's life.

Regular Delivery of Social Services

The not-for-profit status granted to organizations helps them to embark on charity projects and social services delivery. This status is recognized by the civil law, accords tax-exempt status to such organizations. Therefore, it behooves the beneficiary of such status to engage regularly in community development efforts for which it received the tax-exempt status from the government.

The NCC obtained its 501c3 as a nonprofit organization in 2016 and carried out some charity events, but not at a regular mode. Often, planning rather than an unwillingness to embark on these charity events bedevil the organization. It is imperative to create long term planning and schedules for those events so that NCC can maintain regular delivery of social services.

Quarterly Meetings to Review Feedback

In line with the principles of Action Research and Double-loop learning, creating opportunities for the exchange of views can benefit the organization. Double-loop learning creates an environment where individuals can confront one another's views, question the fundamental design and goals of their organizations, and become internally committed to achieving those goals because they arose from participants' free and informed choices (Argyris, 1976). Putting information from feedback into consideration when formulating organizational goals will increase members' commitment to the identified tasks. The NCC conducted a general survey at the beginning of 2019 calendar year to see the opinions of members about the organization. Feedback from those questionnaires was quite revealing and it has helped in reshaping the goals of the organization. Organizing general meetings quarterly was one of the suggestions from the questionnaire and the NCC can achieve more progress by holding such meetings.

The suggested action steps took into consideration Lewin's Action Research or PCM and the Social Transformation Theory (STT). The proposed best practices are also practical answers to the three research questions. They responded to the question about the organizational improvement of an FBO to help is collaborate better with other nonprofit organizations for community development without losing the faith-oriented identity of the organization.

Conclusion

The need for an improvement in the Nigerian Catholic Chaplaincy in Central Ohio, as an FBO, prompted this research. Prior to the choice for the topic, my doctorate journey enlightened me on how to channel academic knowledge towards the improvement of my organization. As a Church minister, I could not effectively channel this knowledge towards changing the entire Catholic Church, but I thought I could start with my little community. I previously worked on the implementation of organizational changes in my workplace as using Lewin's Field Theory as my theoretical framework.

Similarly, Lewin's Action Research/Planned Change Model became the logical theoretical framework for this research. I related more with Lewin's inter-group relationship because he encouraged deep research in order to develop organizational improvement plans. Lewin himself was an immigrant who lived in the diaspora, reminiscing on his challenging society as a Jew in Poland during the Second World War. I combined Lewin's concept with Social Transformation Theory as my two theoretical frameworks because STT dealt with migration and the best practices for effective integration in a diverse society.

Applying Lewin's change model to the research questions seemed logical in addressing my research questions. It gave me the tools to incorporate the change model into my workplace by first analyzing my organization, validating my assumptions through this research process, and gaining support from members of the organization. The unfreezing stage was what the first research question attempted to do. The changing and moving stage was the goal of the second research question, while the refreezing and stabilizing stage was the implication of the third research question. The compelling themes that emerged from data analysis answered these questions.

The data collected from participants during the one-on-one interviews and the focus group discussions surprised me. My researcher's bias had led me to imagine that members of the organization were more eager for rural and community development in Nigeria, due to the volume of remittances Nigerians in the diaspora made to their country of origin. It turned out that the people wanted first to accomplish human and community development here in the United States before venturing into the same goals in Nigeria. The interview responses opened my eyes to these facts, which essentially affected the topic of my research. Their viewpoint was one that I could relate to as someone that shared the same background as diaspora Nigerians, which was the reason my role in the research was as a participant observer.

The analysis of interview data was a daunting task at the beginning, trying to find the right codes and themes to represent adequately what the respondents intended by the answers to the interview protocol. Gradually, through the processes of horizontalization, triangulation, and member checking, validated compelling themes finally emerged from the data. The themes represented, to large extent, what the respondents intended as they affirmed in the final focus group meeting.

Indeed, self-actualization, sense of the sacred and communal spirit are concepts that would resonate with diaspora Nigerians or even Africans everywhere. Moreover, the themes incontrovertibly synchronized with my theoretical frameworks and answered my three research questions. Again, while analyzing data in the research, I was surprised at the near perfect alignment of the compelling themes to my three research questions and ultimately to the research topic itself. A tripartite division of the research topic seemed to have envisioned the compelling themes that emerged from the data analysis. This was the most surprising thing to me during the entire process.

Finally, results from the research have shown that traditionally, Africans are deeply religious in their culture. It does not necessarily arrogate preeminence of piety or better moral standards to Africans than other races, but African people, for the most part, do not know how to exist without religion. Gathering for worship in the chaplaincies and having community events are integral to the way of life of Africans. These events, with their religious undertones, operate as unspoken social coping mechanisms in the African society. As such, Africans in the diaspora try to recreate this society wherever they reside to help them in achieving successful integration into their new society. Nigerian Catholic Chaplaincies mirror the traditional African societies and form these faith-based groups to fulfill the people's religious needs, although attending to the social aspects of their lives is necessary too. Therefore, NCCs must maintain such organizational structure that can carry out the social roles effectively while maintaining the faith-oriented nature of the organization. This way, the organization can play key roles in collaborating with other FBOs toward social services delivery and community development efforts in the society where they live.

BIBLIOGRAPHY

Achebe, C. (1958). *Things fall apart.* Oxford: Heinemann.

Adelman, C. (1993). Kurt Lewin and the origins of action research. *Educational Action Research,* 1(1), 7-24. DOI: 10.1080/0965079930010102

ADPC. (2010). *Annual Report. The Hague, Netherlands: African Diaspora Policy Center.*

ADPC. (2012). *Case Studies of Good Practice in Diaspora Development. Edited Case Studies for Presentation and Discussion at the 2nd African Diaspora Expert Meeting,* Paris.

ADPC. (2013). *Annual Report.* The Hague, Netherlands: African Diaspora Policy Center.

Agunias, D. R., & Newland, K. (2012). *Developing road map for engaging diasporas in development: A handbook for policymakers and practitioners in home and host countries.* Washington, DC: Migration Policy Institute.

Aman, M. (Ed.). (2014). *Diaspora organizations as strategic agents of development.* The Hague, Netherlands: African Diaspora Policy Center.

Argyris, C. (1976). Single-loop and double-loop models in research on decision making. *Administrative Science Quarterly, 21*(3), 363-375.

Awojobi, O. N., Tetteh, J., & Opoku, S. (2017). Remittance, migration and development: Investigating African diaspora in Germany. *International Journal of Innovative Research and Development, 6*(6), 32-38. DOI: 10.24940/ijird/2017/v6/i6/JUN17009

Bielefeld, W., & Cleveland, W. S. (2013a). Defining faith-based organizations and understanding them through research. *Nonprofit and Voluntary Sector Quarterly, 42*(3), 442-467. DOI: 10.1177/0899764013484090

Bielefeld, W., & Cleveland, W. S. (2013b). Faith-based organizations as service providers and their relationship to government them through research. *Nonprofit and Voluntary Sector Quarterly, 42*(3), 468-494. DOI: 10.1177/0899764013485160

Budabin, A. C. (2014). Diasporas as development partners for peace? The alliance between the Darfuri diaspora and the Save Darfur Coalition. *Third World Quarterly, 35*(1), 163–180, http://dx.doi.org/10.1080/01436597.2014.868996

Burchardt, M. (2013). Faith-based humanitarianism: Organizational change and everyday meanings in South Africa. *Sociology of Religion, 74*(1), 30-55. doi:10.1093/socrel/srs068

Carnegie Council. (2016). The other side of migration. *Global Ethics Network.* Retrieved from https://www.carnegiecouncil.org/programs/arc hive/gen

Castles, S. (2010). Understanding global migration: A social transformation perspective. *Journal of Ethnic and Migration Studies,* 36(10), 1565-1586. DOI:10.1080/1369183X. 2010.489381

Castles, S., & Miller, M. J. (2009). *The age of migration: International population movements in the modern world* (4th ed.). New York, NY: The Guilford Press.

Castles, S., de Haas, H., & Miller, M. J. (2013). *The age of migration: International population movements in the modern world* (5th ed.). New York, NY: The Guilford Press.

Charmaz, K. (2006). *Constructing grounded theory: A practical guide through qualitative analysis.* Thousand Oaks, CA: Sage.

Coghlan, D., & Brannick, T. (2014). *Doing action research in your own organization* (4th ed.). Thousand Oaks, CA: Sage.

Creswell, J. W. (1998). *Qualitative inquiry and research design: Choosing among five traditions.* Thousand Oaks, CA: Sage.

Creswell, J. W. (2003). *Research design: Qualitative, quantitative, and mixed methods approaches* (2nd ed.). Thousand Oaks, CA: Sage.

Creswell, J. W. (2007). *Qualitative inquiry and research design: Choosing among five approaches* (2nd ed.). Thousand Oaks, CA: Sage.

Creswell, J. W., & Creswell, J. D. (2018). *Research design: Qualitative, quantitative, and mixed methods approaches* (5th ed.). Thousand Oaks, CA: Sage.

Cummings, T. G., & Worley, C. G. (2009). *Organizational development and change* (9th ed.). Mason, OH: South-Western Cengage Learning.

Davis, C., Jegede, A., Leurs, R., Sunmola, A., & Ukiwo, U. (2011). *Comparing religious and secular NGOs in Nigeria: Are faith-based organizations distinctive?* [Working paper]. International Development Depart., Univ. of Birmingham, Birmingham, UK. Retrieved from: http://www.religionsanddevelopment.org/files/ resourcesmodule/@random454f80f60b3f4/ 1300096101_working_paper_56_complete_for _web.pdf DOI: ISBN: 9780704428720

De Lange, J. (2016). *What is organizational restructuring and how will it influence the growth of the firm?* Retrieved from https://specialties.bayt.com/en/ specialties/q/266784/what-is-organizational- restructuring-and-how-will-it-influence-the- growth-of-the-firm/

de Haas, H. (2010). The internal dynamics of migration processes. A theoretical inquiry. *Journal of Ethnic and*

Migration Studies, 36(10), 1587-1617. DOI: 10.1080/1369183X.2010.489361

de Haven, M. J., Hunter, I. B., Wilder, L., Walton, J. W., & Berry, J. (2004). Health programs in faith-based organizations: Are they effective? *American Journal of Public Health, 94*(6), 1030–1036.

Dodani, S., & LaPorte, R. E. (2005). Brain drain from developing countries: How can brain drain be converted into wisdom gain? *Journal of the Royal Society of Medicine, 98*(11), 487-491. DOI: 10.1258/jrsm.98.11.487

Duff, J. F. (2010). *Many faiths, common action: Increasing the impact of the faith sector on health and development.* Washington, DC: Center for Interfaith Action on Global Poverty. Retrieved from http://www.cifa.org

Duggan, T. (2018). How can one incorporate Kurt Lewin's theory of work? Article in *azcentral.com.* Retrieved from https://yourbusiness.azcentral.com/can-one-incorporate-kurt-lewins-theory-work-13946.html

Ekeke, C. E., & Ekeopara, C. (2010). Gods, divinities, and spirits in African traditional religious ontology. *American Journal of Social and Management Sciences, 1*(2), 209-218. DOI: 10.5251/ajsms.2010.1.2.209.218

Enyi, J. E. (2014). Rural and community development in Nigeria: An assessment. *Arabian Journal of Business and Management Review, 2*(2), 17-30.

Eylon, D. (1998). Understanding empowerment and resolving its paradox: Lessons from Mary Parker Follett. *Journal of Management History,* 4(1), 16-28.

French, W. L., & Bell, Jr. C. H. (1999). *Organizational development: Behavioral science interventions for organizational improvement* (6th ed.). Upper Saddle River, NJ: Prentice-Hall.

Golafshani, N. (2003). Understanding reliability and validity in qualitative research. *The Qualitative Report,* 8(4), 597-606.

Gordon, A. (1998). The new diaspora African immigration to the United States. *Journal of Third World Studies, 15*(1), 79-103.

Gsir, S., & Mescoli, E. (2015). Maintaining national culture abroad – countries of origin, culture and diaspora. *INTERACT RR 2015/10*. Retrieved from http://www.eui.eu/RSCAS/Publications/

Hargreaves, A., & Fullan, M. (2012). *Professional capital: Transforming teaching in every school*. New York, NY: Teachers College Press.

Hartzell, S. (2018). Lewin's 3-stage model of change: Unfreezing, changing, & refreezing. *Lesson Transcript from Business 101: Principles of Management.* Retrieved from https://study.com/academy/lesson/lewins-3-stage-model-of-change-unfreezing-changing-refreezing.html

Hepworth, C., & Stitt, S. (2007). Social capital and faith-based organizations. *The Heythrop Journal,* 48(6),

895-910.   DOI: 10.1111/j.1468-2265.2007.00348.x

Hesser-Biber, S. N., & Leavy, P. (2011). *The practice of qualitative research* (2nd ed.). Los Angeles, LA: Sage.

ICMPD. (2013). *Migration and development policies and practices: A mapping study of eleven European countries and the European commission.* Vienna, Austria: International Center for Migration and Policy Development.

Idang, G. E. (2015). African culture and values. *Phronimon,* 16(2), 97-111.

Joshi, P., Hawkins, S., & Novey, J. (Eds.). (2008). *Innovations in effective compassion: Compendium of research papers presented at the faith-based and community initiatives conference on research, outcomes, and evaluation.* Washington, DC: U.S. Department of Health and Human Services.

Kessing, L. L., & Marquard-Busk, U. (2014). *Diaspora – Mediating actors in development: A case study about Somali diasporas in Denmark. Research Brief.* The Hague, Netherlands: African Diaspora Policy Center.

Khondker, H. H., & Schuerkerns, U. (2014). Social transformation, development and globalization, 1-14. *Sociopedia.isa.* DOI: 10.1177/205684601423

Kindanka, C. (2016, November). Saint or not, Nyerere led an exemplary life. *The East African.* Retrieved from https://www.theeastafrican.co.ke/magazine/Sai

nt-or-not-Nyerere-led-an-exemplary-life--/434746-3441810-c9762w/index.html

Levine, J. M., & Hogg, M. A. (Eds.). (2010). *Encyclopedia of group processes and intergroup relations.* Thousand Oaks, CA: Sage.

Lincoln, Y. S., & Guba, E. G. (1985). *Naturalistic inquiry.* Newbury Park, CA: Sage.

Lincoln, Y. S., & Guba, E. G. (2000). Paradigmatic controversies, contradictions, and emerging confluences. In N. K. Denzin & Y. S, Lincoln (Eds.), *Handbook of qualitative research* (2nd ed., pp. 163-188). Thousand Oaks, CA: Sage.

Locke, L. F., Silverman, S. J., & Spirduso, W. W. (2010). *Reading and understanding research* (3rd ed.). Thousand Oaks, CA: Sage.

Maslow, A. H. (1970). *Motivation and personality.* New York, NY: Harper & Row.

Maxwell, J. A. (2005). *Qualitative research design: An interactive approach* (2nd ed.). Thousand Oaks, CA: Sage.

Mbiti, J. S. (1989). *African religions and philosophy* (2nd ed.). Oxford: Heinemann.

McHenry, D. E. (1980). Ujamaa villages: The implementation of a rural development strategy. *The Journal of Modern African Studies,* 18(4), 703-704.

Merrigan, G., & Huston, C. L. (2015). *Communication research methods* (3rd ed.). New York, NY: Oxford University Press.

Mind Tools Team. (2018). Lewin's change management model: Understanding the three stages of change. Retrieved from https://www.mindtools.com/article/newPPM_94.htm

Newland, K., Terrazas, A., & Munster, R. (2010) Diaspora philanthropy: Private giving and public policy. Washington, D.C: Migration Policy Institute.

Nyerere, J. K. (1987). Ujamaa: The basis of African socialism. *The Journal of Pan African Studies,* 1(1), 4-11.

Ojo, S. (2012). Ethnic enclaves to diaspora entrepreneurs: A critical appraisal of Black British Africans' transnational entrepreneurship in London. *Journal of African Business,* 13(2), 145-156. DOI: 10.1080/15228916.2012.693446

Onwubiko, O. A. (1991). *African thought, religion, and culture.* Enugu: SNAAP Press.

Pratt, C. (1999). Julius Nyerere: Reflections on the Legacy of His Socialism. *Canadian Journal of African Studies / Revue Canadienne Des Études Africaines,* 33(1), 137-152. DOI:10.2307/486390

Raheem, W. M., & Bako, A. I. (2014). Sustainable rural development programmes in Nigeria: Issues and challenges. *Asian Journal of Science and Technology,* 5(9), 577-586.

Roberts, C. M. (2010). *The dissertation journey: A practical and comprehensive guide to planning, writing, and defending your dissertation* (2nd ed.). Thousand Oaks, CA: Sage.

Rogers, R. K. (2009). Community collaboration: Practices of effective collaboration as reported by three urban faith-based social services programs. *Social Work & Christianity* 36(2), 326-345.

Schein, E. H. (1992). *Organizational culture and leadership* (2nd ed.). San Francisco, CA: Jossey-Bass.Terrazas, A. (2010). *Connected through service: Diaspora volunteers and global development.* Washington, D.C: Migration Policy Institute.

Thompson, L. L. (2008). *Organizational behavior today.* Upper Saddle River, NJ: Pearson Prentice-Hall.

Tinajero, S. P. A., & Sinatti, G. (2011). *Migration for development: A bottom-up approach. A handbook for practitioners and policymakers.* Brussels, Belgium: EC-UN Joint Migration and Development Initiative (JMDI). Retrieved from http://www.globalmigrationgroup.org/system/f iles/uploads/UNCT_Corner/theme7/jmdi_augu st_2011_handbook_migration_for_developme nt.pdf

Turner, S., & Kleist, N. (2013). Introduction: Agents of change? Staging and governing diasporas and the African State. *African Studies,* 72(2), 192-206.

Udu, L. E., & Onwe, S. E. (2012). Approaches to community development in Nigeria, issues and challenges: A study of Ebonyi State community and social development agency. *Journal of Sustainable Development,* 9(1), 296-307. DOI:10.5539/ jsd.v9n1p296.

United Nations Population Fund. (2009). *Guidelines for engaging faith-based organizations (FBOs) as agents of change*. New York: UNFPA.

Urban Dictionary. (2016). Retrieved from https://www.urban dictionary.com/define.php?term=kinsmanship

Vidal, A. C. (2001). *Faith-based organizations in community development*. Washington, DC: U.S. Department of Housing and Urban Development.

Weiss, R. S. (1994). *Learning from strangers: The art and methods of qualitative interview studies*. New York, NY: The Free Press.

Williams, M. L. (2010). *Diasporic awakenings: Mobilizing diasporas for homeland causes* (Doctoral dissertation). Department of Political Science, University of Washington.

Zimmer, C. (2016, September 22). How we got here: DNA points to a single migration from Africa. *The New York Times*. Retrieved from: https://www.nytimes.com/2016/09/22/science/ ancient-dna-human-history.html

APPENDICES

Appendix A

Interview Protocol for One-on-one Interviews

1. What is your name?
2. What is your date of birth?
3. What is your marital status?
4. Do you have children? How many? Give their age(s).
5. Any other family members living with you or resident in the United States?
6. Where do you live?
7. When did you arrive in the United States? (How long have you been in the United States?)
8. What was your purpose and aspirations coming into the United States?
9. Have they been achieved or are being achieved?
10. Describe your experiences integrating into the American society.
11. Did it affect your relationship with family and friends back in Nigeria?
12. Are you employed? If yes, what is the nature of your employment?
13. Is your annual income (a) above $100,000? (b) below $100,000 but above $60,000? (c) below $60,000 but above $30,000?
14. Do you give to charity in general? What percentage or amount annually?
15. Do you make remittances to family or friends back home in Nigeria? What percentage or amount annually?

16. How is your current relationship with family and friends back home in Nigeria? (Have your views changed toward supporting them and have theirs developed in terms of dependence/independence over the years?).

17. Are you involved in any community development efforts, here in the United States or Nigeria?

18. What is your opinion about collective efforts toward community development in Nigeria, by the NCC?

19. What is your perception about NCC? What roles would you like to see the organization play in your life and in the Nigerian Catholic Chaplaincy here in the USA?

20. How is the NCC currently organized to undertake this role

21. As a member of the NCC, in what ways do you think the organization can be improved to perform better towards community development in Nigeria?

22. If a spiritual role was included in the responses to #18, what are your suggestions for improvement?

23. Do you belong to any other organization or social group? Name them.

24. Does any of them help with community development in Nigeria?

25. Do they work in collaboration with any government or not-for-profit agency?

26. How can NCC be organized to collaborate better with government or not-for-profit agencies towards community development in Nigeria?

27. Any other thoughts or reflections you wish to share about these ideas?

Appendix B

Focus Group Protocol

1. What is your opinion about collective efforts toward community development in Nigeria by the NCC?

2. What is your perception about NCC? What roles would you like to see the organization play in your life and in the Nigerian Catholic community?

3. How is the present organization of NCC equipped to undertake this role?

4. If not, in what ways can the organization be improved to perform better towards community development in Nigeria?

5. If spiritual role was included in the responses to #2, what are your suggestions for improvement?

6. Do you know of other Nigerian organizations or social groups here in the United States that are involved with community development in Nigeria?

7. Do they work in collaboration with any government or not-for-profit agency?

8. How can the NCC be organized to collaborate better with government or not-for-profit agencies towards community development in Nigeria?

9. Any other thoughts or reflections you wish to share about these ideas?

Appendix C

Matrix of Initial Codes

Codes	Haifa	Vin	Viber	Freddick	Winner
Self-improvement		Came to study, have a career, and take care of myself, p. 2	I came to study, to obtain a degree in business and go back home to help improve our people, p. 1	I arrived to study so that I could return to Nigeria and continue serving the government that sent me to the US, p. 1	We came to go to school, pp. 2, 3
Planned/positive integration	I know my way around, I know how things work…" p. 2	"I was in school for 9 years, got my PhD, and I'm enjoying being able to take care of myself" pp. 1-2.	It was a shock, to say the least, beginning with the weather. Instructional method at school was challenging too, p. 2	Prior biases from stories and news magazines about reckless shootings. Realized there are very friend-ly people in US, p. 3	We did research before coming to the US to know which School to attend, p. 4

Accent and integration				I had to get used to the way they speak their English, p. 3	They start making fun of you, the way you talk. pp. 4, 5
Self-reliance.	I know my way around, I know how things work…there hasn't been much difficulty, p. 3	"I liked the idea of being independent." p. 1-2. "It wasn't much of a big deal" pp. 1-2.	I adjusted very quickly and then integrated into the society, p. 2	In about a month or two I got used to the American accents, p. 3	"They started understanding the stuff we were made of" p. 4. Integration was so easy.
Sense of entitlement		They bug you with phone calls for money… nobody calls you form home to ask how you are… In general, they think that you pluck money from trees, p. 4		As soon as I got a job, it was like I shall solve all their problems for them, p. 4	"the only friendship is money. That's the connection"; p. 9 If you don't send them money, they say you have forgotten them; p. 9
Community devpt. efforts	Contributing to education, health, skills	Many things that could be done at home where our	I feel grateful to God for what I am	It's something worth doing but we have to get	I volunteer in places here to do community

	develop-ment, business, training, and even general assistance, pp. 5, 9, 10, 11	government are not doing anything, p. 11	today, and I feel I have to give back to the society, p. 4, 5, 8	the struc-tures right first. You have to ensure that the gifts get to the intended people, p. 8	work. E.g.. Food banks p. 10. In Nigeria, I assist, women, elderly people, and children, p. 10, p.25
Collective effort toward devpt.	I think it's a good idea a good incen-tive be-cause… there a lot of things our people need back there in Nigeria… that are not being met by the govt. p. 4	I think it's a great thing to do if we can. The church is supposed to be the leader for doing these kinds of things, p. 8, 14. We have talents within our community to be tapped, p. 14	Believes in and is involved in collective efforts toward develop-ment with town's people. "We provided electricity to the entire village" pp. 5, 6, 7	I don't have any commu-nity efforts here in America. I make per-sonal dona-tions to different organiza-tions, p. 7.	It's great idea but problematic - tribalism
Tribal sentiment	Why don't you do the project in my hometown?	It just boils down to the same problem of tribalism we have in Nige-			If I say let's do it, are you going to do it in Enugu, Anambra, or

	p. 10	ria... pp. 10-11, 13			Imo? p. 12
Collaborate with non-profit organization		We can use the resources/ talents we have to write grants and source for funds, p. 14			
Spiritual role, by NCC		Spiritual nourishment and protection of our values, p. 9	I would like the NCC to continue to strengthen my faith, p. 6	The NCC fulfills my faith need by situating our worship in our own cultural way of doing so in Nigeria, p. 10.	To deepen my spiritual life
Social role by NCC	To provide support, moral support in good and bad times, p. 5 Information sharing.	We are all immigrants, in a very far away land. NCC should be like a home in a foreign place, p. 8		We need to have a little bit of home flavor in the community here, to care of the nostalgic feelings p. 9	To strengthen marriage & family life

Sense of belonging		For me, NCC is like another home where you come together, discuss your issues, cele-brate joys and share sorrows together, p. 8 United Nigeri-anness, p. 12		That sense of belonging I get it from my Nigerian Catholic community, p. 10.	When I come (for Nig. Mass) I feel like I'm at home in Nigeria, p. 18
Self determi-nation	To integrate into the society, get a job and start con-tributing my own part to society, p. 2	What drove me to this part of the world was studies, so that I could have a career and be independent, p. 2			
Good relationship with family	Very good, cordial. In constant contact. p. 3	The only relative at home was mum and I had great relation-ship with her, p. 4	We were in touch and have remained in touch, p. 2		Great relationship with family. p. 9

Charitable spirit	I give to charity. Gave away all my belongings when I relocated to the US, p. 3	Apart from my donations to church and needy persons, I still help people who cannot afford the fees in my professional career, p. 5	What inspires me to keep giving and not count the cost is that we also grew up in abject poverty, p. 3	Personal donations to different organiza-tions, like the Cancer Society and the Catholic relief organi-zation, p. 8	I would say every year we give up to $20,000 in charity
Communal spirit	I think it's important to support family and friends and this view of mine will not change anytime soon. As we are living in the diaspora, we have to supply the needs of the people back home, p. 4	Every now and then, there is a death or some-thing like that back home, we send them money to support, p.6	Before I came here, I got a phone call from home of some relative who needs to bury a family member and it involves money. I will give and I'm not going to write it down anywhere,	10% of my earnings go to help family members back home, p. 5 A death in the family means a big chunk of money to be contributed, p. 5	I have a project I started with about 10 women, where I give them 10,000 naira each, to start something doing. They return it over some years and the money is

			pp. 3, 5		given to other women, etc. p. 11
Organizational structure	Good leadership and information hub, p. 6	I think we are organizationally structured well, p. 9		I would want us to be fully organized… and then go for fund drive, p. 13	If we can have groups to be in charge different aspects of projects, p. 17
Information hub	Part of the things the NCC needs to do is information sharing, where it would be a hub for information, pp. 6, 7, 8, 9 & 17				
Identity	Inculcate our history to the children so they don't				

	get passive about their origin, p. 7				
Self-funded Projects by NCC	Rather than donate to NGOs we can go directly and do something, p. 14		In the social organization where I belong, out funds are member-generated funds, p. 10	More numbers of members, more money, p. 9	
Financial reality (amidst unrealistic expectations from home)		There is so much bills to pay. Even if you make a lot of money here, they are still going into paying the bills, pp. 4-5		The money you make is taxed so much and from it you still squeeze out something just to help out back in Nigeria, p. 4	
Need for numerical strength		Not all of us Nigerian Catholics are coming out, pp. 8, 9, 10, 15		We have to campaign more to get more members, pp. 9, 10, 13	The attendance is very poor. Conduct a survey to find out

					why, p. 19
Self-image				Because my name is on the line, being the first child int the family. Expectations they have of me is high. If you don't meet some of these expec-tations, it's like you are a nobody; p. 6	
Accountability			They kept receipts and good records of every penny we sent, to our amazement, p. 6	Making sure the help gets to those that need it. We have that issue of trust in Nigeria, p. 9	
Discrimina-tion outside of the community				At my regular parish, I wouldn't know who	

				wants to shake hands or not. It's not supposed to be that way, p. 11.	

Globethics.net Publications

The list below is only a selection of our publications. To view the full collection, please visit our website.

All products are provided free of charge and can be downloaded in PDF form from the Globethics.net library and at www.globethics.net/publications. Bulk print copies can be ordered from *publictions@globethics.net* at special rates for those from the Global South.
Paid products not provided free of charge are indicated[*].
The Editor of the different Series of Globethics.net Publications is Prof. Dr Obiora Ike, Executive Director of Globethics.net in Geneva and Professor of Ethics at the Godfrey Okoye University Enugu/Nigeria.

Contact for manuscripts and suggestions: *publications@globethics.net*

Global Series

Christoph Stückelberger / Jesse N.K. Mugambi (eds.), *Responsible Leadership. Global and Contextual Perspectives*, 2007, 376pp. ISBN: 978–2–8254–1516–0

Heidi Hadsell / Christoph Stückelberger (eds.), *Overcoming Fundamentalism. Ethical Responses from Five Continents*, 2009, 212pp.
ISBN: 978–2–940428–00–7

Christoph Stückelberger / Reinhold Bernhardt (eds.): *Calvin Global. How Faith Influences Societies*, 2009, 258pp. ISBN: 978–2–940428–05–2.

Ariane Hentsch Cisneros / Shanta Premawardhana (eds.), *Sharing Values. A Hermeneutics for Global Ethics*, 2010, 418pp.
ISBN: 978–2–940428–25–0.

Deon Rossouw / Christoph Stückelberger (eds.), *Global Survey of Business Ethics in Training, Teaching and Research*, 2012, 404pp.
ISBN: 978–2–940428–39–7

Carol Cosgrove Sacks/ Paul H. Dembinski (eds.), *Trust and Ethics in Finance. Innovative Ideas from the Robin Cosgrove Prize*, 2012, 380pp.
ISBN: 978–2–940428–41–0

Jean-Claude Bastos de Morais / Christoph Stückelberger (eds.), *Innovation Ethics. African and Global Perspectives*, 2014, 233pp.
ISBN: 978–2–88931–003–6

Nicolae Irina / Christoph Stückelberger (eds.), *Mining, Ethics and Sustainability*, 2014, 198pp. ISBN: 978–2–88931–020–3

Philip Lee and Dafne Sabanes Plou (eds), *More or Less Equal: How Digital Platforms Can Help Advance Communication Rights*, 2014, 158pp. ISBN 978–2–88931–009–8

Sanjoy Mukherjee and Christoph Stückelberger (eds.) *Sustainability Ethics. Ecology, Economy, Ethics. International Conference SusCon III, Shillong/India*, 2015, 353pp. ISBN: 978–2–88931–068–5

Amélie Vallotton Preisig / Hermann Rösch / Christoph Stückelberger (eds.) *Ethical Dilemmas in the Information Society. Codes of Ethics for Librarians and Archivists*, 2014, 224pp. ISBN: 978–288931–024–1.

Prospects and Challenges for the Ecumenical Movement in the 21st Century. Insights from the Global Ecumenical Theological Institute, David Field / Jutta Koslowski, 256pp. 2016, ISBN: 978–2–88931–097–5

Christoph Stückelberger, Walter Fust, Obiora Ike (eds.), *Global Ethics for Leadership. Values and Virtues for Life*, 2016, 444pp. ISBN: 978–2–88931–123–1

Dietrich Werner / Elisabeth Jeglitzka (eds.), *Eco-Theology, Climate Justice and Food Security: Theological Education and Christian Leadership Development*, 316pp. 2016, ISBN 978–2–88931–145–3

Obiora Ike, Andrea Grieder and Ignace Haaz (Eds.), *Poetry and Ethics: Inventing Possibilities in Which We Are Moved to Action and How We Live Together*, 271pp. 2018, ISBN 978–2–88931–242–9

Christoph Stückelberger / Pavan Duggal (Eds.), *Cyber Ethics 4.0: Serving Humanity with Values*, 503pp. 2018, ISBN 978–2–88931–264-1

Texts Series

Principles on Sharing Values across Cultures and Religions, 2012, 20pp. Available in English, French, Spanish, German and Chinese. Other languages in preparation. ISBN: 978–2–940428–09–0

Ethics in Politics. Why it Matters More than Ever and How it Can Make a Difference. A Declaration, 8pp, 2012. Available in English and French. ISBN: 978–2–940428–35–9

Religions for Climate Justice: International Interfaith Statements 2008–2014, 2014, 45pp. Available in English. ISBN 978–2–88931–006–7

Ethics in the Information Society: The Nine 'P's. A Discussion Paper for the WSIS+10 Process 2013–2015, 2013, 32pp. ISBN: 978–2–940428–063–2

Principles on Equality and Inequality for a Sustainable Economy. Endorsed by the Global Ethics Forum 2014 with Results from Ben Africa Conference 2014, 2015, 41pp. ISBN: 978–2–88931–025–8

Water Ethics: Principles and Guidelines, 2019, 41pp. ISBN 978–2–88931–313–6, available in three languages.

Praxis Series

Christoph Stückelberger, *Responsible Leadership Handbook: For Staff and Boards*, 2014, 116pp. ISBN :978-2-88931-019-7 (Available in Russian)

Angèle Kolouchè Biao, Aurélien Atidegla (éds.,) *Proverbes du Bénin. Sagesse éthique appliquée de proverbes africains*, 2015, 132pp. ISBN 978-2-88931-068-5

Elly K. Kansiime, *In the Shadows of Truth: The Polarized Family*, 2017, 172pp. ISBN 978-2-88931-203-0

Christopher Byaruhanga, *Essential Approaches to Christian Religious Education: Learning and Teaching in Uganda*, 2018, 286pp. ISBN: 978-2-88931-235-1

Christoph Stückelberger / William Otiende Ogara / Bright Mawudor, *African Church Assets Handbook*, 2018, 291pp. ISBN: 978-2-88931-252-8

Oscar Brenifier, *Day After Day 365 Aphorisms*, 2019, 395pp. ISBN 978-2-88931-272-6

Christoph Stückelberger, *365 Way-Markers*, 2019, 416pp. ISBN: 978-2-88931-282-5 (available in English and German).

Benoît Girardin / Evelyne Fiechter-Widemann (Eds.), *Blue Ethics: Ethical Perspectives on Sustainable, Fair Water Resources Use and Management*, forthcoming 2019, 265pp. ISBN 978-2-88931-308-2

Elly Kansiime, *Theology of Work and Development*, 158pp. 2020, ISBN 978-2-88931-373-0

Theses Series

Kitoka Moke Mutondo, *Église, protection des droits de l'homme et refondation de l'État en République Démocratique du Congo*, 2012, 412pp. ISBN: 978–2–940428–31–1

Ange Sankieme Lusanga, *Éthique de la migration. La valeur de la justice comme base pour une migration dans l'Union Européenne et la Suisse*, 2012, 358pp. ISBN: 978–2–940428–49–6

Kahwa Njojo, *Éthique de la non-violence*, 2013, 596pp. ISBN: 978–2–940428–61–8

Carlos Alberto Sintado, *Social Ecology, Ecojustice and the New Testament: Liberating Readings,* 2015, 379pp. ISBN: 978-2–940428–99–1

Symphorien Ntibagirirwa, *Philosophical Premises for African Economic Development: Sen's Capability Approach*, 2014, 384pp. ISBN: 978–2–88931–001–2

Jude Likori Omukaga, *Right to Food Ethics: Theological Approaches of Asbjørn Eide*, 2015, 609pp. ISBN: 978–2–88931–047–0

Jörg F. W. Bürgi, *Improving Sustainable Performance of SME's, The Dynamic Interplay of Morality and Management Systems*, 2014, 528pp. ISBN: 978–2–88931–015–9

Jun Yan, *Local Culture and Early Parenting in China: A Case Study on Chinese Christian Mothers' Childrearing Experiences,* 2015, 190pp. ISBN 978–2–88931–065–4

Frédéric-Paul Piguet, *Justice climatique et interdiction de nuire*, 2014, 559 pp. ISBN 978–2–88931–005–0

Mulolwa Kashindi, *Appellations johanniques de Jésus dans l'Apocalypse: une lecture Bafuliiru des titres christologiques*, 2015, 577pp. ISBN 978–2–88931–040–1

Naupess K. Kibiswa, *Ethnonationalism and Conflict Resolution: The Armed Group Bany2 in DR Congo.* 2015, 528pp. ISBN: 978–2–88931–032–6

Kilongo Fatuma Ngongo, *Les héroïnes sans couronne. Leadership des femmes dans les Églises de Pentecôte en Afrique Centrale*, 2015, 489pp. ISBN 978–2–88931–038–8

Bosela E. Eale, *Justice and Poverty as Challenges for Churches: with a Case Study of the Democratic Republic of Congo*, 2015, 335pp, ISBN: 978–2–88931–078–4

Andrea Grieder, *Collines des mille souvenirs. Vivre* après *et avec* le génocide *perpétré contre les Tutsi du Rwanda*, 2016, 403pp. ISBN 978–2–88931–101–9

Monica Emmanuel, *Federalism in Nigeria: Between Divisions in Conflict and Stability in Diversity*, 2016, 522pp. ISBN: 978–2–88931–106–4

John Kasuku, *Intelligence Reform in the Post-Dictatorial Democratic Republic of Congo*, 2016, 355pp. ISBN 978–2–88931–121–7

Fifamè Fidèle Houssou Gandonour, *Les fondements éthiques du féminisme. Réflexions à partir du contexte africain*, 2016, 430pp. ISBN 978–2–88931–138–5

Nicoleta Acatrinei, *Work Motivation and Pro-Social Behaviour in the Delivery of Public Services Theoretical and Empirical Insights*, 2016, 387pp. ISBN 978–2–88931–150–7

Timothee B. Mushagalusa, *John of Damascus and Heresy. A Basis for Understanding Modern Heresy*, 2017, 556pp. ISBN: 978-2-88931-205-4

Nina, Mariani Noor, *Ahmadi Women Resisting Fundamentalist Persecution. A Case Study on Active Group Resistance in Indonesia*, 2018, 221pp. ISBN: 978-2-88931-222-1

Ernest Obodo, Christian *Education in Nigeria and Ethical Challenges. Context of Enugu Diocese*, 2018, 612pp. ISBN: 978-2-88931-256-6

Fransiska Widyawati, *Catholics in Manggarai, Flores, Eastern Indonesia*, 2018, 284pp. ISBN: 978-2-88931-268-9

A. Halil Thahir, *Ijtihād Maqāṣidi: The Interconnected Maṣlaḥah-Based Reconstruction of Islamic Laws*, 2019, 200pp. ISBN 978-2-88931-220-710

Tibor Héjj, *Human Dignity in Managing Employees. A performative approach, based on the Catholic Social Teaching (CST)*, 2019, 320pp. ISBN: 978-2-88931-280-1

Sabina Kavutha Mutisya, *The Experience of Being a Divorced or Separated Single Mother: A Phenomenological Study*, 2019, 168pp. ISBN: 978-2-88931-274-0

Florence Muia, *Sustainable Peacebuilding Strategies. Sustainable Peacebuilding Operations in Nakuru County, Kenya: Contribution to the Catholic Justice and Peace Commission (CJPC)*, 2020, 195pp. ISBN: 978-2-88931-331-0

Mary Rose-Claret Ogbuehi, *The Struggle for Women Empowerment Through Education*, 2020, 410pp. ISBN: 978-2-88931-363-1

Nestor Engone Elloué, *La justice climatique restaurative: Réparer les inégalités Nord/Sud*, 2020, 198pp. ISBN 978-2-88931-379-2